RAW VEGAN MEALS

Recipes for healthy eating

Scott Mathias

I would like to dedicate this book to the growing number of people who are adopting a vegan lifestyle and thereby helping our beautiful planet earth to become a better place for all sentient beings.

A very special and heartfelt mention of my partner, Clare Darwish, without whom, much of what I achieve in my busy day would not happen. Her drive and insistence on 'living the passion', has helped mould this book and also helped create the first of what we see as many GoVegan Delis around the world. Also a further mention of our wonderful foundation staff in our first store, Yas, Hiro, Sandra, Nina and Auriel – without whom the growing 'wave' of food awareness would remain just a mere ripple on the shoreline of our ever changing lives. Thank you.

CONTENTS

Introduction

When I began my own healing journey little did I know it would manifest into what can only be described as a 'most amazing life'.

This is my third publication, my second recipe book and I am overwhelmed with gratitude and love for this new opportunity to share my raw vegan alchemic skills, imagination and creativity with you.

Working my magic into boxes and on to platters and boards, has opened up a new dimension of 'food freedom' – the amalgam of flavors and colors, the veneration of what I eat and most importantly, the sharing of raw vegan food from not just modern platters but also ancient timber boards and bowls.

My work as a raw food chef and digestive health specialist continues as people seeking a vegetarian or vegan lifestyle, increases unabated. I believe this to be, quite simply, because old world foods – meat, wheat, dairy, processed foods, grains and white sugar – no longer nourish our bodies. I eat none of those foods.

I have proven beyond doubt, the food I eat determines my gene purity and the quality of physical and intellectual wellbeing. I no longer need to be 'tested' on the facts. Now into my 63rd year, I can report I enjoy wonderful health and now have totally detached from the day-to-day media preoccupation with 'painful and premature death as an inevitability'. This is not my reality.

In the many talks and raw vegan food demonstrations I do, I talk about detaching from the old and worn out matrix of human life and finding the courage to recreate 'a new matrix of being' – which entails eating high frequency, solar-filled, live food for the living body. I am able to report that adopting this approach to living will change your perspective on reality to one of greater love for all things, greater caring for all things and above all, greater compassion for all things. Love – Care – Compassion: the three plinths supporting a foundation of awareness, which I know is healing the Physical-Body and Earth-Body simultaneously.

What is within is with-out. Put in simple terms; when I changed the frequency of my body through the food I chose to use to heal myself, then the frequency of my surroundings became more positive and supportive.

I send you my love if you are just starting out in your healing journey. I made it a short trip so I could spend more time living my purpose and enjoying the wonderful life experiences, which come my way daily. It's your choice too if you wish to prolong the journey or fast track by removing all food which does nothing to support an empowered life.

Here's to your wonderful health and a new and healthy future for our home called EARTH – HEART.

What is raw vegan food?

I only came across the words raw and vegan a decade ago. I grew up living with almost 100% animal products and lived 45 years of illness as my gut rebelled against meat and dairy products along with wheat and all its gluten based derivatives.

I lived with an inflamed body and mind, and a soul detached from the true meaning of being, which I now know is living a happy, pain-free, productive and purposeful life.

The actual word 'vegan' is derived from the word VEG-etari-AN and was coined in 1944 by Donald Watson when he co-founded the Vegan Society in England. At first it meant 'non-dairy vegetarian' and later the doctrine 'man should live without exploiting animals'.

Raw vegan food is entirely plant based and uncooked so as not to destroy the all-important nutrients. Plant based food can be dehydrated but at a temperature of no more than 42.5°C (115°F). After this the nutritional value begins to diminish.

My food lifestyle is free of the following:
- Meat
- Wheat and wheat products, including pasta
- Dairy, including yogurt
- Processed food of any nature
- Grains, including dried or cooked beans
- Rice, because it turns to sugar in my digestive system
- Eggs, because they are derived from an animal
- Honey, because it is derived from an insect
- White sugar, which in my honest opinion, has the same capacity to get us hooked as heroine

At this stage, I will point out that all of this food had a terrible affect on me from a very early age. I spent much of my life skirting around the plate looking for edible vegetables – most of which were boiled and over-cooked – until I realised uncooked, fresh, organic vegetables and fruit suited my nutritional disposition.

What I realise now is wholly plant based eating helps the body stay alive. Since starting this lifestyle, and I mean 'lifestyle' as opposed to a diet, my life has changed so profoundly; I am at a loss for words to describe the miracles that I have attracted to me.

Implements and aids to create raw vegan food

If you are a new raw vegan and still finding your way around recipes and implements then I would love to refer you to my *Let's Eat Raw* recipe book because it contains a full and comprehensive list of things you will need to successfully 'eat your way through your day'.

However I will provide a condensed version of that list here to get you started:
- Medium to large wooden chopping block
- A sharp, medium-sized knife
- A two-cup personal blender
- Optional: Larger high-speed blender
- Optional: S-blade food processor
- Optional: Dehydrator with 5-9 trays

Your oven will also double as a dehydrator when set at its lowest temperature, 40–50°C (110–130°F) with the fan on and the door open. Any reference in the recipe line-up to dehydration will relate to the use of a traditional dehydrator. If using an oven to dry fruit or vegetables it is advisable to cut the drying time by half and remain vigilant ensuring over-drying doesn't occur.

What is food in a box, on a platter or board?

I have eaten 'Japanese food in a box – bento style' on and off during my life. I just love its 'compartmentalised' form and beautiful presentation or range of mouth-watering morsels. It is food presented in a box – round, oval or square; large, medium or small – depending on your appetite or the occasion.

Now I enjoy eating this way whenever I can. Sharing this approach with you and members of the public provides an opportunity to venerate the food, dutifully provided to us by planet Earth. The opening of our first GoVegan Deli is a testament to the growing demand for food served this way.

Bento's origins are distinctly Japanese and go back centuries when the emperors were delivered their lunch and evening snacks in boxes. Over the years eating this way has become almost a daily pursuit for the modern Japanese with special boxes being used for different occasions.

I recall as a child going to school, my lunch in a brown paper bag filled with an assortment of goodies all wrapped up in greaseproof paper. In those days the food wasn't seen as being appropriate or not, it was just food. My favorite sandwich was cold beef spaghetti bolognaise between two slabs of white bread. I may have enjoyed the taste but soon after my gut was writhing – gluten and meat served me no good. Back then no-one took the time to think those two food items were contributing to my digestive woes. Along with the sandwich was normally a large slice of my dear mother's fruitcake, full of flour and butter – adding to the pain of eating. Then there might have been a lump of cheese, which definitely hit the mark at the base of my gullet adding to the appearance in my late teens of a hiatal hernia, an associated condition bought on by continual amounts of acid and liquid food being spontaneously ejected from my pained gut. However, my mother would spice up the daily offering with other goodies such as pieces of carrot and celery, wrapped singularly to add to the gift-like, 'unwrapping' experience. These usually went down well but in no way compensated for the pain experienced as a result of the other food.

Point being, I still loved the 'surprises', which according to my research, indicates that many Japanese people still enjoy when they pick up their daily bento box from their local railway station. They might be starved for time but the Japanese never go hungry – eating food is a very important part of their daily life.

In short, bento or 'food in a box' is not just restricted to Japanese food. You will find in this book a myriad of national foods and recipes, which I use regularly – Thai, Indian, Italian, Moroccan and Mexican are all my favorites. I hope they will become yours too.

The power of the 'food platter'

Without a proper and balanced daily diet of 'living food' the body will ultimately meet an untimely demise – food will either harm you or heal you. Food presented beautifully on a platter to be shared with family and friends is sure to cure most ills.

Food contained in vessels made from some of Earth's fundamental elements such as wood or metal, not only present well but taste better. What I have created in this recipe book is raw plant based food, full of flavor, which meets a frequency supporting a long, happy, healthy, productive and pain-free life.

Food either served directly from a platter or bowls on a platter, has been shown scientifically to not only look better but also taste better – beautiful and attentive presentation makes a real difference. You will see from the wonderful images in this book exactly what we are alluding to. An Oxford University Gastrophysicist, Professor Charles Spence actually led a team, which found that:

"Even with such basic dishes, thoughtful presentation meant diners found the food more flavorful: simply serving cucumber thinly sliced on top of the other salad ingredients, made the dish considerably more appetising."[1]

My raw food approach is simply based on the following, using all vegan plant based ingredients – vegetables, fruits and nuts:

- Sweet
- Sour
- Salty
- Savory
- Creamy
- Crunchy

My box, platter or board contains what appeals to me at the time of my meal. What is in my fridge may also determine the make-up of my food. In recent days, my desire for more fermented foods has increased markedly; so too many others who share their daily food intake stories with me. The gut loves fermented food because it helps to maintain a 'good gut biome' or flora. You will find lots of fermented vegetables on my daily menu – I will show you how you can create them simply, quickly and easily with no-fuss.

Simple raw vegan boards – 'less is the new more'

Whatever composition or approach you'd like to take to create your own 'board' of raw food, whether it be for 'in-house' consumption, for the workplace or even school, then go with your heart because I find the food I select is exactly the food my body needs at that time.

I see not only 'veneration' through the use of boxes, platters and boards but also community – when people sit down together 'sharing' takes on a completely new meaning; put beautiful food into bowls or onto pieces of flat timber and watch your diners light up with expectation and conversation.

The Spanish have taken the use of boards and bowls in serving food to great heights. Tapas – literally meaning 'to cover' – originated in Spain, where according to legend, King Alfonso X, The Wise King of Spain, once stricken with serious illness could only take in small portions of food with small amounts of wine. To this day tapas is a major part of Spanish food style and like the Japanese bento box, has been exported throughout the world.

In this book I share my recipes by the box, platter or board; a different approach to starters, entrees, mains and desserts. The idea being that you can try any of the recipes for any of the combinations and when you have mastered them you can create any combination you desire. ENJOY!

Health giving qualities of vegetables

Mushrooms are so easy to marinate and once you have made up the marinade you can just keep adding to it with fresh Portobello or Swiss Brown button mushrooms. They are high in vitamin B12, vitamin D and renowned for their anti-inflammatory and immune enhancing qualities.

Spinach is high in vitamin K, vitamin A and magnesium along with a myriad of other properties, including 11% protein.

Peas are your zinc go-to vegetable.

Cauliflower, a 240 g (8.5 oz) serving contains 77% of the recommended daily (RDA) value of vitamin C. It's also a good source of vitamin K, protein, thiamin, riboflavin, niacin, magnesium, phosphorus, fiber, vitamin B6, folate, pantothenic acid, potassium and manganese.

Carrots contain vitamin A and the anti-oxidant betacarotene. Both are recognized for the regenerative and immunological characteristics. It also has a traditional quality recognized by most mothers around the world – it is supposed to be good for improving eyesight, being high in vitamin A.

White Cabbage, just eating 170 g (6 oz) of even cooked cabbage would provide 47% of your vitamin C needs for the day. It also provides 102% of vitamin K, 8% of manganese, 6% of folate and lesser amounts of vitamin B-6, calcium, potassium and thiamine.

Red Cabbage is high in vitamin A, vitamin K, vitamin C and iron. The red color also contains the antioxidant anthocyanin comprising of lutein and zeaxanthan, which is known to be beneficial to eye health.

Tomatoes are an excellent source of vitamin C, biotin, molybdenum and vitamin K. They are also a very good source of copper, potassium, manganese, dietary fiber, vitamin A (in the form of beta-carotene), vitamin B6, folate, niacin, vitamin E and phosphorus. Consumption of tomatoes has been linked to optimum prostate health.

Cacao, the darker the chocolate the higher the antioxidant levels. Cacao contains high bioflavonoid levels that may facilitate healthy blood flow and blood pressure levels. Eating foods with a high percentage of cacao may help prevent the clogging of arteries, thereby reducing risk of stroke, blood clots and heart attacks.

Almonds are one of the complete sources of energy as well as nutrients. They are rich in mono-unsaturated fatty acids like oleic, and palmitoleic acids that have shown to help in lowering LDL or 'bad cholesterol' and increasing HDL or 'good cholesterol'. They are also high in non-gluten proteins and throwing a handful into your breakfast daily may assist with cardiovascular health.

Coconut, once demonised, is a wonderful tree nut containing a range of amazing fats in the form of oil. Almost 50% of the fatty acids in coconut oil is the 12-carbon lauric acid. When coconut oil is enzymatically digested, it also forms a monoglyceride called monolaurin. Both lauric acid and monolaurin can kill harmful pathogens like bacteria, viruses and fungi; these are just some of its qualities.

Strawberries are potent little packages known to assist heart health, increase HDL (good) cholesterol, lower blood pressure and guard against cancer. Packed with vitamins, fiber, and particularly high levels of antioxidants known as polyphenols, strawberries are a sodium-free, fat-free, cholesterol-free, low-calorie food. They are among the top 20 fruits in antioxidant capacity and are a good source of manganese and potassium. Just one serving – about eight strawberries – provides more vitamin C than an orange.

Wasabi, a diet rich in wasabi has anti-inflammatory properties, which may offer relief from aching joints. It helps inhibit inflammatory pathways, which may lead to inflammation. In particular it is the action of isothiocynates in wasabi that may prevent inflammatory bowel disease as well as asthma.

Dulse flakes (seaweed) contain vitamins A, B1, B2, B3, B6, B12, C and E, and minerals like potassium, calcium, magnesium, phosphorous, chromium, iodine and zinc and trace elements. It is a wonderful naturally occurring food 'supplement'.

Nutritional savory yeast is a source of B vitamins, including thiamine, folate, B-6 and niacin. Just half a tablespoon of some brands will provide you with a day's worth of B vitamins, while other brands offer between 30 and 100% of B vitamins. These vitamins help you extract the energy from food and produce red blood cells. Many types of nutritional yeast are also fortified with vitamin B-12, which is usually found exclusively in animal products. For vegans, fortified nutritional yeast thus becomes a source of this nutrient.

Asian Fusion

I am fortunate enough to have chosen to live in one of the most magnificent parts of this beautiful planet. Here all the wonderful spices used in Thai food grow in abundance – garlic, ginger, galangal, kaffir lime leaf, green limes and coriander (cilantro) – I find these spices exciting not the least because of their pungency and natural fragrance. You will find these delightfully aromatic and tasty spices throughout this book. The combination is simple and storable, particularly the mushrooms and carrot kimchi.

Menu

Corn Spinach And Green
Pea mash Pinwheels

·

Marinated Button
Mushrooms

·

Baby Tomatoes

·

Cauliflower Rice Sushi

·

Quick Carrot Kimchi

·

Red And White Cabbage
Noodles In Asian Kaffir
Lime Sauce

Corn, Spinach and Green Pea Mash Pinwheels

It is not mandatory to include the cashew cream as the straight pea and spinach combination is just as tasty.

Ingredients for the wraps:

750 g (26 oz) frozen organic corn kernels, thawed (frozen seem to work better than using fresh ones)

500 g (16 oz) fresh English spinach, washed

1 teaspoon onion salt (store-bought, free of anticaking agents is preferred)

125 g (4 oz) ground flaxmeal

60 g (2 oz) ground psyllium husks

Extra water if needed

Ingredients for the green pea mash:

500 g (16 oz) frozen organic peas, thawed

250 g (8 oz) fresh English spinach leaves, chopped

½ medium clove fresh garlic

¼ teaspoon sea salt

¼ teaspoon ground pepper

2 dessertspoons cashew cream (see page 22)

Method for the wraps:

1. Place the corn, spinach and onion salt into an S-bladed food processor and blend thoroughly. Add the flaxmeal and psyllium and continue to blend until mix falls away from the sides. If the mix is too dry add a small amount of water to achieve the desired consistency.
2. Using a small stainless flat headed spatula make 22 cm (9 in) squares on baking paper or heat resistant teflex paper (commonly used in dehydrators). This mix will make approx. 2–4 wraps, depending on the size of your tray.
3. Place in a dehydrator on a temperature of 42.5°C (115°F) for 6 hours, turning end to end each hour. Do not over dry. A flexible moist wrap will fill easily when rolled.
4. When drying is complete cut off any rough or dried edges to create a nice square shape.

Method for the green pea mash:

1. Blend all the ingredients until a coarse consistency is obtained.

Method for the pinwheels:

1. To the previously prepared green pea mash add 2 dessertspoons of cashew cream. Stir together with a spoon. Set aside the balance of the cream for future use.
2. Place 3–4 dessertspoons of the combined pea and cream mixture on to the wraps keeping 3 cm (1 in) of the top of the wrap (furthest away from you) free of the mix. Roll the wrap away from you and add some water to the last 3 cm (1 in), which will enable it to stick to the roll. It is now ready for slicing into 3–4 cm (1 in) pieces. Cut on an angle to provide an interesting effect.

Cashew Cream

Ingredients for the cashew cream:

In a two-cup blender:

Fill ⅓ of the blender with raw cashew nuts

Fill ⅔ of the blender with coconut cream

¼ clove of garlic

¼ teaspoon lime juice, to taste

¼ teaspoon sea salt, to taste

¼ teaspoon ground pepper, to taste

Method for the cashew cream:

1. Blend thoroughly until smooth.
2. Add coconut water if you would like the mix thinner.
3. Cream stored in a glass jar will last up to seven days.

Marinated Button Mushrooms

Ingredients:

36 cleaned button mushrooms (Portobello or Swiss Brown have the best flavor)

125 ml (4 fl oz) olive oil

60 ml (2 fl oz) apple cider vinegar

3 dessertspoons coconut palm syrup

1 glove of garlic

salt and pepper, to taste

Method:

1. Place the cleaned mushrooms in a large jar. Add all the other ingredients making sure the mix is sweet enough. Add more coconut syrup if desired.
2. Set aside for 4–6 hours, turning every hour. The outcome will be beautifully marinated whole mushrooms ready to serve. These will stay in good edible condition for up to 3 weeks.

Baby Tomatoes

Often just plain vegetables fit the bill when it comes to preparing your box or platter. I love anything 'baby' when it comes to vegetables, especially, and now I reveal a total bias, TOMATOES. In particular, colored cherry tomatoes including some of the heirloom varieties, which have made a comeback to the market place.

This selection includes zebras, jelly beans, vine ripened cherries, yellows and straight cherry tomatoes. They bring so much color to any plate or box – I enjoy slightly dampening my tomatoes and lightly sprinkling them with my beautiful earth salt. You may also choose to lightly drizzle your favorite olive oil, apple cider vinegar or lime juice over them as well. Either way the wonderful tastes of these gorgeous creations of nature will burst forth, filling the mouth with joyful flavors.

Cauliflower Rice Sushi

Ingredients:

½ medium size cauliflower

½ avocado

½ teaspoon of mirin (fermented rice seasoning) or Japanese vinegar

1 spring onion (scallion) or shallot, finely chopped

3–4 sheets of Nori (Japanese seaweed paper)

125 g (4 oz) pea sprouts, for garnish

Method:

1. Pulse the cauliflower in a food processor until rice-like in consistency. Add the finely chopped shallots or spring onions and about half of the avocado flesh. Pulse together to achieve a sticky consistency.

2. Place a piece of the Nori paper shiny side up on your chopping block and spoon on the prepared cauliflower mixture leaving around 3 cm (1 in) clear at the head of the paper. Smooth out the cauliflower mix being sure not to use too much otherwise it will become difficult to roll. Wet the remaining strip of paper and continue to roll letting the 'wetted' area stick to the body of the sushi roll. You can use a sushi mat if you wish in order to get greater firmness.

3. Slice into 3 cm (1 in) pieces and garnish with pea sprouts.

Quick Carrot Kimchi

Kimchi is traditionally made in Korea and contains either a shrimp or fish sauce. It is essentially a cured cabbage, which becomes more intense in flavor the longer it remains in storage. In Korea most families gather once or twice a year to make kimchi together.

Ingredients:

4 carrots, finely sliced
3 limes, juiced
3 dessertspoons apple cider vinegar
½ red chili, finely chopped
½ teaspoon chopped ginger
1 teaspoon desert salt
½ teaspoon ground pepper

If you wish to make a lot of kimchi just increase the other ingredients proportionally and add:
⅛ teaspoon vegetable fermenting culture (L-Platarum)

Method:

1. Around 2-3 hours in advance, put the carrots through the dicing attachment on your food processor, turning out into a prep bowl. Thoroughly massage all the ingredients together adding more lime juice and salt to taste. Set aside in a bowl or jar.
2. Just before serving thoroughly massage once again and place the 'squeezed' vegetables onto a serving platter. Serve at room temperature.
3. If adding the fermenting culture, then the vegetables can be stored in jars for up to 4 weeks before eating. Always refrigerate the jars after opening.

Red and White Cabbage Noodles in Asian Kaffir Lime Sauce

....

Ingredients for the Asian kaffir lime sauce:

cashew cream sauce, left over from your pinwheels (see page 22)

¼ teaspoon freshly ground ginger root

⅛ teaspoon galangal (a member of the ginger family but more 'rooty' in appearance with a more pungent fragrance)

1 kaffir lime leaf, de-veined (tear both sides of the leaf away from the center stem)

1 lime, juiced

2 dessertspoons of coconut water

earth salt, to taste

Ingredients for the noodles:

¼ red cabbage, sliced finely

¼ white cabbage, sliced finely

½ red capsicum (bell pepper), finely sliced

2 limes, juiced

¼ teaspoon earth salt

¼ teaspoon ground pepper, to taste

Method for the Asian kaffir lime sauce:

1. Thoroughly blend all ingredients for 30 seconds or so to achieve a very creamy consistency. Taste test and add earth salt if necessary.

Method for the noodles:

1. Place the sliced cabbage and capsicum mixture into a prep bowl and pour over the kaffir lime sauce. Thoroughly blend together and let sit for an hour or so. The lovely limey flavors from the kaffir will fully merge with the cabbage creating an awesome eating experience.

Fresh Flavors

Your box does not have to be either
complicated or filled to capacity. Some
years ago I adopted the 'less is more'
attitude and quickly found I was just as
satiated; remember nutrient dense foods
fill your stomach very quickly, so one
doesn't need as much volume anymore.

Menu

Vine Ripened Tomatoes
With Kaffir Lime Cream Cheese

•

Zucchini Noodle And Coriander
Salad With Pineapple Chili
Dressing

•

Hemp Corn Salad With Spicy
Coconut Flakes And Hazelnuts

•

Green Papaya And Cabbage
Quick Kimchi

Vine Ripened Tomatoes with Kaffir Lime Cream Cheese

Ingredients for the cream cheese:

250 g (8 oz) raw cashew nuts
250 ml (8 fl oz) coconut cream
60 ml (2 fl oz) coconut oil
1 kaffir lime leaf, deveined
1 small clove of garlic
½ teaspoon freshly squeezed
   lime juice
2 cm (0.8 in) fresh ginger,
   peeled
1 cm (½ in) galangal, peeled
¼ teaspoon desert salt, to taste
⅛ teaspoon ground pepper

Ingredients for the tomatoes:

2 medium tomatoes, with tops
   removed
2 golden shallots or spring
   onions (scallions), thinly
   sliced
6 capers
2 dessertspoons virgin olive oil
3 dessertspoons red wine
   vinegar or apple cider vinegar
   with a slice of beetroot
   soaked for a few minutes to
   create red wine vinegar effect
1 clove of garlic, crushed
Micro greens, to garnish

Method for the cream cheese:

1. The day before, combine all the ingredients in a high-speed blender until a thick creamy consistency is achieved. Pour off into a prep bowl and refrigerate over night or until firm but soft consistency.
2. The next day spoon into a piping bag until full and place back into the refrigerator to maintain firmness until ready to use. This makes it easier to fill the tomato – otherwise use a teaspoon.

Method for the tomatoes:

1. Cut around the top of the tomato and scoop out the interior. Combine the shallots and capers with the oil, vinegar and crushed clove of garlic. Fill the tomato with the cheese and top off with the shallots, caper and garlic mixture.

Zucchini Noodle and Coriander Salad with Pineapple Chili Dressing

....

Ingredients for the zucchini noodles and coriander salad:

2 medium sized zucchini (courgette), peeled and spiralised (use a hand spiraliser or easy to operate 3 in 1 bench-top machine)

500 g (16 oz) red cabbage, sliced thinly

1 medium white turnip, peeled and finely diced

1 sheet nori roll paper, cut into small squares

60 g (2 oz) raw cashew nuts (roasted and salted are acceptable)

60 g (2 oz) coriander (cilantro), coarsely cut (set aside some leaves for garnish)

2 red shallots or spring onions (scallions), thinly sliced

Ingredients for the pineapple chili dressing:

2 Birdseye or Jamaican chilies (or chili of choice), coarsely chopped, or 2 teaspoons of dried chili pieces

2 medium garlic cloves, coarsely chopped

250 g (8 oz) fresh sweet pineapple, diced into small pieces

3 limes, juiced

salt and pepper, to taste

Method:

1. Combine all the salad ingredients in a prep bowl.
2. Combine all the dressing ingredients and mix.
3. Toss the dressing into the salad and serve. Garnish with remaining coriander leaves.

Hemp Corn Salad with Spicy Coconut Flakes and Hazelnuts

Ingredients for spicy coconut flakes:

500 g (16 fl oz) coconut flakes (available from your health food store)

60 ml (2 fl oz) wheat-free tamari

1/8 teaspoon smoked paprika

1/8 teaspoon cardamom

1/8 teaspoon cinnamon

1/8 teaspoon cayenne pepper

Ingredients for the salad:

2 medium corncobs, kernels removed

125 g (4 oz) hulled hemp seeds, soaked for 2 hours

60 g (2 oz) spicy coconut flakes (recipe above)

60 g (2 oz) raw hazelnuts, coarsely chopped

2 shallots or spring onions (scallions), finely chopped

1 lime, juiced

Ingredients for the nut parmesan garnish:

250 g (8 oz) finely crushed macadamia nuts

2 dessertspoons nutritional yeast

1 teaspoon chopped chives, for garnish

salt and pepper to taste

You may also like to use cashews to make a nut parmesan.

Method for spicy coconut flakes:

1. Thoroughly mix all ingredients together until the coconut flakes are totally coated.
2. Place on a dehydrating tray (or baking paper on baking tray) and dry for 3–4 hours until flakes are crisp and dry. A reminder that if you are using your oven as a dehydrator then set temp on lowest possible, with fan on and door open and expect drying time to be halved. Either way check periodically, turning and mixing through to ensure continuity of drying until nice and crisp.

Method for finished salad:

1. Thoroughly combine all the salad ingredients.
2. Combine the nut parmesan ingredients and sprinkle over the top of the salad with the chives to complete the taste experience.

Green Papaya and Cabbage Quick Kimchi

This is another approach to this very traditional Korean accompaniment.

Ingredients:
½ peeled and seeded medium green papaya, sliced into 5 cm (2 in) strips

½ white cabbage, finely sliced

½ red cabbage, finely sliced

6 limes, juiced

125 ml (4 fl oz) apple cider vinegar

1 medium chili, finely chopped

1 teaspoon caraway seeds

½ teaspoon desert salt

½ teaspoon ground pepper

Method:
1. Combine all ingredients, thoroughly massaging the papaya and cabbage. Add more lime juice and salt to taste. Set aside for 3–4 hours.
2. Just before serving thoroughly massage once again and place the 'squeezed' vegetables into a prep bowl ready for placing into your box, or into a larger serving dish.

Mexican Fiesta

If you are a mother concerned about what to put into your child's lunch box then select a few of these items and make it fun. I know so many children who just love kale chips and walnuts as a crunchy alternative. If there is a 'no nuts of any kind' policy at your child's school then replace the walnuts in the following recipe with sunflower seeds, soaked and slightly pulsed in your food processor.

Menu

Spicy Corn Salsa

•

Baja Kale Chips

•

Guacamole

•

Zarangollo –
'No Roast' Capsicum With Pimento

•

No-Refried Beans

•

Zucchini And Corn Tortillas
With Nueces Molidas And Sour
Nut Cream

Spicy Corn Salsa

Ingredients:

kernels from 2 fresh corn cobs
1 red onion, quartered
6 large tomatoes, halved
1 red capsicum (bell pepper), quartered
1 red chili, finely chopped
¼ teaspoon smoked paprika
2 pickled gherkins
2 dessertspoon coriander (cilantro), shredded
2 limes, juiced
2 teaspoons of olive oil
salt and pepper, to taste

Method:

1. Place all the ingredients except the corn in your food processor. Pulse until a lumpy puree consistency is reached. I like my salsa quite chunky. Taste for extra seasoning.

2. Turn into a prep bowl adding in the corn kernels. Stir through and transfer to a small container which can either stand in your box or at the side as an accompaniment. Garnish with a few leaves of coriander. You can also use this as a filling for your tortilla.

Baja Kale Chips

Ingredients:

1 large bunch of washed Russian or curly leaf kale

½ sweet pineapple, skinned, de-cored and chopped

1 red capsicum (bell pepper), chopped

½ fresh red chili, chopped

1 teaspoon sea salt

Method:

1. De-vein and strip the kale into bite size pieces and set aside.
2. In your blender, add the pineapple, capsicum, chili and salt and pulse down to a puree consistency. Pour the mixture onto the deveined kale and work thoroughly through with your fingers. Once totally covered in the marinade, lay the pieces of kale out on teflex or baking paper.
3. Set the temperature to 42°C (115°F) on your dehydrator or if using an oven bring the temperature up until the light just comes on, leave the door open and fan on. Dehydrating will take 6–10 hours, or the oven will take 3–5 hours depending on the efficiency of the appliances. You are looking for a nice crispy outcome.
4. A note of warning; do your best not to be tempted to eat them all at once!

Guacamole

Ingredients:

4 ripe avocados, de-stoned

125 g (4 oz) coriander (cilantro)

2 limes, juiced

¼ fresh green chili

1 medium clove garlic

½ red onion

salt and pepper, to taste

Method:

1. Add all the ingredients to your food processer and blend until smooth, or to the consistency preferred. Place this in a bowl separately in your box or serve in your tortilla.

Zarangollo – 'No Roast' Capsicum with Pimento

Ingredients:

6 red capsicums (bell peppers), cut into strips

125 ml (4 fl oz) olive oil

60 ml (2 fl oz) apple cider vinegar or red wine vinegar

2 limes, juiced

1 red chili, finely chopped

60 ml (2 fl oz) coconut palm nectar crystals

3 garlic cloves, chopped finely

salt and pepper, to taste

60 g (2 oz) parsley, flat or English, finely chopped

½ teaspoon smoked sweet paprika

Method:

1. Prepare the capsicums by liberally dousing the strips in olive oil, vinegar, lime juice, chili and coconut palm nectar. Add the garlic and ¼ of a teaspoon of salt along with a good grind of pepper and let sit in the marinade overnight.

2. The next morning, remove the capsicum from the marinade and turn into a prep bowl. Add the finely chopped parsley and paprika, drizzle in some of the leftover marinade and serve as an accompaniment to your tortilla.

No-Refried Beans

....

Ingredients:

300 g (10 oz) sprouted chickpeas (precooked canned chickpeas are OK, the raw food police are not breathing down your neck!)

350 g (12 oz) sunflower seeds, soaked for 3–4 hours

125 ml (4 fl oz) olive oil

2 teaspoons wheat free tamari

1 teaspoon dried onion powder (available from your supermarket's herb and spice shelf)

½ red chili

1 medium clove of garlic

1 teaspoon cumin powder

1 teaspoon nutritional or savory yeast

salt and pepper, to taste

Method:

1. Blend all the ingredients in your food processor until a 'refried bean' consistency is reached. Turn out into a serving bowl. Add to your tortilla or serve in a separate container or with chopped lettuce leaves.

Nueces Molidas (Walnuts in Tomato Sauce)

Just a reminder, the same outcome can be achieved using sunflower seeds.

Ingredients:

500 g (16 oz) walnuts, soaked for 2 hours

3–4 medium organic tomatoes

250 g (8 oz) sun- or semi-dried tomatoes

2 tablespoons lime or lemon juice

½ fresh chili, add more or less based on your preference

2 tablespoons cumin powder

2 tablespoons coriander powder

2 tablespoons paprika powder

2 tablespoons garlic powder, or 2 large garlic cloves, pressed

1 teaspoon oregano powder

2 teaspoons salt

¼ teaspoon ground pepper

Method:

1. Using your food processor, pulse blend the walnuts then add the balance of the ingredients. You are looking for a chunky, familiar 'mince like' consistency; do your best to not over-process the walnuts. The final outcome is a great protein and nutrient alternative to mince. Can be served on its own with accompaniments.

Zucchini and Corn Tortillas

Ingredients:

4 medium zucchini
   (courgettes), peeled
kernels from 2 fresh corn cobs
   (equivalent in frozen is OK)
125 g (4 oz) psyllium powder
2 tablespoons fresh garlic,
   crushed
1–2 teaspoons onion powder,
   depending on your taste
   preference
1 tablespoon turmeric powder
170 g (6 oz) flaxmeal, ground
2 teaspoons salt
¼ teaspoon ground black
   pepper
480 ml (16 fl oz) water

Method:

1. Blend the zucchini and corn until smooth and then add the balance of the ingredients.
2. Slowly add in the water keeping some in reserve to adjust consistency for spreading onto teflex sheets or baking paper. It might take you several attempts to achieve this. Be assured, practice makes perfect.
3. Spread a layer approx. 3–4 cm (1 inch) in size onto your heat resistant paper, ensuring there are no holes. Set the dehydrator to 42.4°C (115°F) or put the oven on less than 50°C (122°F), fan on and door open for 2–3 hours. Take care not to fully dry the tortillas, as you need to be able to fold them. It is better to turn them over at the halfway mark, simply by flipping the entire sheet and peeling it off the tortilla.
4. Fill your tortillas with the nueces molidas, sour nut cream, spicy corn salsa and no-refried beans.

Sour Nut Cream

Ingredients:

250 g (8 oz) raw cashews,
   soaked for 3–4 hours
2 limes, juiced
2 dessertspoons nutritional
   savory yeast
1 medium clove of garlic,
   peeled and crushed
salt and pepper, to taste

Method:

1. Combine all the ingredients in a blender until a creamy consistency is achieved. Feel free to use lemons if limes are not available. Lemons will achieve a more sour flavor.

Raw Vegan Sushi

In the last 20 years planetary food cultures have all become ubiquitous – available almost everywhere. Sushi is one such cuisine to come out of Japan which is now 'everywhere' on Earth. This fusion box is one of my favorite combinations because they are all 'little bites' bursting with flavor. Also great for school and office lunches and if heat from the wasabi isn't to your liking then just leave it out.

Menu

Daikon Sushi with
Cauliflower Rice and
Avocado, Sunflower Seed
Mock Tuna, Creamy Wasabi
Mayonnaise and ginger

·

Spicy Pickled Vegetables

·

Spicy Vegetable Wraps
With Peanut Dipping Sauce

·

Tomato and Carrot Sushi
Wrap

·

Garden Peas with Radish
and Watercress Greens

·

Brassica Noodles with
Peanut Sauce

Daikon Sushi with Cauliflower Rice and Avocado, Sunflower Seed Mock Tuna, Creamy Wasabi Mayonnaise and Pickled Ginger

Ingredients for rice and avocado:

2 medium daikon radish (zucchini (courgettes) will also suffice)

½ cauliflower, chopped into florettes

½ avocado, flesh removed

2 dessertspoons sushi wine

1 teaspoon fresh wasabi or ½ teaspoon mock wasabi in a tube

1 teaspoon lime juice

wheat free tamari (light soy sauce), to serve

salt and pepper, to taste

Ingredients for pickled ginger:

250 g (8 ¾ oz) fresh ginger root, peeled and sliced

250 ml (8 ¾ fl oz) apple cider vinegar

2 tablespoons agave syrup

salt and pepper, to taste

Method for rice and avocado:

1. Place the cauliflower in a food processor and, using the pulse function, reduce to a rice-like consistency.
2. Using a prep bowl, gradually add the avocado, sushi wine, wasabi and lime juice. Take care not to make the mixture too wet or too hot with wasabi. Taste as you go.
3. Blend entire ingredients so the avocado has a chance to bind the cauliflower rice together. Too much avocado makes it too sticky and difficult to work with.
4. You can choose to leave the wasabi out and serve it separately if you wish.
5. Using a mandolin thinly slice the peeled daikon. Lay one of the slices down on your chopping board and gently place a layer of the mixture over the top. Roll and pin together with a toothpick. If you do not have a mandolin, which can be purchased quite cheaply from a kitchen shop, then finely slice with a sharp knife. Some old-fashioned cheese graters have a flat side, which can also be used to grate the daikon across.
6. Serve with wheat free tamari sauce and pickled ginger (recipe below).

Method for homemade pickled ginger:

1. Peel fresh ginger and run through a mandolin on a thin setting.
2. Place in a bowl and cover with the apple cider vinegar and agave syrup.
3. Add salt and pepper and set aside in a jar for several days.

Ingredients for the mock tuna:

500 g (16 oz) sunflower seeds, soaked overnight

½ teaspoon dried mustard powder (or 1 teaspoon dijon mustard)

3 tablespoons chopped red onion

1 garlic clove, minced, optional

4 tablespoons lemon juice

1 tablespoon capers

1 medium-sized dill pickle

2 tablespoons dulse (seaweed) flakes

salt and pepper, to taste

Ingredients for the creamy wasabi mayonnaise:

150 ml (6 fl oz) coconut cream

1 dessertspoon white barley miso (fermented barley)

2 tablespoons olive oil

1 tablespoon apple cider vinegar

1 tablespoon water

½ lemon, juiced

½ teaspoon pre-made wasabi, or powder to make up

½ teaspoon onion powder

¼ teaspoon salt, to taste

¼ teaspoon ground pepper, to taste

Method for the mock tuna:

1. Combine all the ingredients in a food processor until a 'tuna' type consistency is achieved.
2. Adjust seasoning to suit your pallet.
3. Lay one of the daikon slices down on your chopping board and gently place a layer of the 'tuna' mixture over the top. Roll and pin together with a toothpick. Repeat.
4. Slice and arrange on a serving plate and add some of the creamy wasabi mayonnaise on top to finish.
5. Garnish with chopped parsley or dill.

Method for the creamy wasabi mayonnaise:

1. Place all ingredients in a high-speed blender and process, being sure to scrap down the sides, until mixture is smooth.
2. You may choose to add a crushed garlic clove to this for extra flavor.

Spicy Pickled Vegetables

Ingredients:

2 medium carrots, peeled and julienned

1 medium white turnip, peeled and julienned

200 g (7 oz) green or snake beans, finely diced

60–125 g (2–4 oz) fine sea salt crystals

3 limes, juiced

1 teaspoon kaffir lime leaves, chopped finely

1 medium chili finely diced

125 g (4 oz) coriander (cilantro) leaves, finely chopped

1 dessertspoon coconut palm syrup

1/4 teaspoon ground pepper

Method:

1. Place the julienned carrots, turnip and beans in a glass bowl with the salt. Add just enough water to cover the vegetables. Set aside for 2–4 hours. The solution should taste quite salty but do vary the amount of salt based on personal preference.

2. When you are ready, rinse the vegetables off in a sieve and put into a prep bowl. Add the lime juice, kaffir lime leaves, chili, coriander and splash of coconut palm syrup. Add salt and pepper as required. Place into a serving dish and they ready to enjoy.

3. These vegetables also lend themselves to being stored in an airtight container in the refrigerator. Serve with a tasty salad or spicy tropical food.

Spicy Vegetable Wraps With Peanut Dipping Sauce

Ingredients:

Leaves from green vegetables to act as cups for your filling

2 medium daikon radish (also known as Japanese radish)

½ red capsicum (bell pepper) thinly sliced into 10 cm (4 in) lengths

4 shallots or spring onions (scallions) thinly sliced into 10 cm (4 in) lengths

½ small cucumber thinly sliced into 10 cm (4 in) lengths

2 medium carrots, peeled and sliced into 10 cm (4 in) lengths

1/2 kaffir lime leaf, vein removed and finely chopped

250 g (4 oz) coriander (cilantro), chopped

½ teaspoon lime juice, squeezed over the prepared vegetables

Ingredients for the dipping sauce:

2 cloves of garlic

½ teaspoon fresh ginger

75 ml (2 fl oz) olive oil

30 ml (1 fl oz) wheat-free tamari sauce

1/2 medium red chili

1 dessertspoon coconut palm syrup, to taste

1 heaped dessertspoon of peanut butter (organic, all natural ingredients)

1–2 limes, juiced, to taste

salt and pepper, to taste

Method:

1. Leaves from greens such as lettuce, spinach, kale, collard, Chinese cabbage or bok choy are acceptable. Remove the ribs of the greens so they fold nicely. Its important to make sure your filling is diced small enough, which makes filling easier.

2. Combine all the other ingredients and set aside ready to be used as the filling for the wrapped leaves.

3. When ready place equal quantities of the vegetables into the chosen leaf layer by layer and roll firmly with the trimmed stem closest to you. Fold together as if you were wrapping a small parcel. Use a toothpick if necessary to hold the wrap together.

Method for the dipping sauce:

1. Blend until everything is thoroughly broken down. Do a final taste test and serve in small dipping dish beside your box or in a small recyclable container.

2. Note: this is a favorite so if you are preparing for a crowd just increase the ingredients proportionally to meet appetite needs. Also serve the sauce in dishes which can accommodate a good handful of vegetable wrap.

Tomato and Carrot Sushi Wrap

Ingredients:

4 large vine ripened tomatoes

2 medium size carrots, peeled

40 g (1 ½ oz) ground flaxmeal

salt and pepper, to taste

Method:

1. Thoroughly blend the tomatoes, carrots and flaxmeal, testing for flavor. You are looking for a thick but flowing consistency where the mix falls away from the side of your blender.

2. Using a stainless steel spatula or pallet knife, smooth up to 5 dessertspoons of the mix onto baking paper or heat resistant teflex paper suitable for a dehydrator. Form an even flat square about 25 x 25 cm (10 x 10 in).

3. Aim for a 5 mm (1/4 in) thickness evenly spread over the paper.

4. Put into the dehydrator at 55°C (140°F) for 60 minutes then turn down to 42.5°C (115°F) for a further 4–5 hours, all the time watching for the mixture to separate from the paper. As soon as this occurs its time to flip the paper over and gently peel it off the drying mixture. The underneath should be moist.

5. Continue to dehydrate for a further 1 hour ensuring the wrap doesn't become too dry.

6. The end product will have reduced to approx. 2 cm (0.8 inch) thick and should be pliable and ready to be used to wrap either vegetables or the 'mock tuna' sushi style.

7. I normally square up the edges to obtain uniformity when wrapping. They will keep up to two weeks in an airtight bag in the fridge.

8. To fill, simply spoon on a layer of the mock tuna to around 5 cm (2 in) high followed by a layer of the creamy mayonnaise.

9. Leave the top of the wrap free of ingredients (furthest end away from you). Begin to roll firmly either by free hand or using a sushi mat. Wipe water along the uncovered end to aid in the sealing process.

10. I normally place the entire roll into the fridge for an hour or so, enabling it to firm up, which makes it easier for cutting.

11. For evenness I firstly cut the wrap in half and then each half in half again.

12. This becomes a very colorful addition to your bento box.

Garden Peas with Radish and Watercress Greens

Ingredients:

2¼ kg (1 lb) fresh garden peas hulled to provide 300–400 g (10.5–14 oz) peas or 400 g (14 oz) thawed organic garden peas

4 red radishes, cleaned and sliced into 'rounds'

½ medium sized white turnip, finely diced

1 teaspoon chopped chives

3 limes, juiced

1 dessertspoon olive oil

1 teaspoon apple cider vinegar

¼ teaspoon desert salt

¼ teaspoon ground black pepper

250 g (8 oz) of cleaned and washed watercress greens

Method:

1. Hull the fresh peas or thaw the frozen peas and place in a bowl with the other ingredients. Mix through and taste to test. Serve on white spoons as a starter or canapé.

2. The amazing flavors will surprise you!

Brassica Noodles With Peanut Sauce

Ingredients for the noodles:

½ Chinese or Wom Bok cabbage, finely chopped to achieve a noodle effect

½ purple cabbage, finely sliced to achieve the appearance of a noodle

1 red capsicum (bell pepper), finely sliced

1 medium red onion

6 sugar snap peas

125 g (4 oz) fresh coriander (cilantro) leaves, chopped

1 dessertspoon macadamia oil

12 fresh coriander leaves, to serve

Ingredients for the peanut sauce:

125 g (4 oz) peanut butter

125 ml (4 fl oz) cashew nut milk (see recipe provided)

80 ml (2.5 fl oz) namu shoyu sauce

1 teaspoon tamarind paste (available from an Asian grocer)

1 medium red chili

1 dessertspoon fresh ginger

1 dessertspoon agave or coconut palm syrup

¼ teaspoon ground black pepper

2 dessertspoons lime juice

Method for the noodles:

1. Place the cabbage along with the rest of the chopped vegetables in a prep bowl adding the coriander. Keep some coriander back for garnish.

Method for the peanut sauce:

1. Blend all the ingredients into a smooth to runny consistency. Add more or less of all ingredients to achieve the outcome that works best with your pallet. Don't forget to 'taste test' as you go.
2. Pour the peanut sauce over the prepared cabbage and thoroughly blend through. Also lovely with pickled vegetables.

Method for cashew nut milk:

1. To make 500 ml (17 fl oz) of pre-made cashew nut milk soak 120 g (4 oz) of raw cashew nuts overnight. The next morning pour off the liquid, place the nuts into a blender and add 480 ml (16 fl oz) of water. Blend thoroughly until a creamy consistency is achieved. Add more or less water depending on preference. This stores well in a glass bottle for up to 4–5 days.

Taste of Morocco and the Med

Some years ago I went through a phase of 'everything Moroccan' and to this day I still maintain a fascination for this part of North Africa – all the fantastic varieties of food and tastes. Throw in a little touch of the southern and western Mediterranean and you have a cacophony of cuisines.

Menu

Lebanese Za'atar
Flat Bread

·

Cauliflower Couscous

·

Fattoush With Hummus

·

Moroccan Gazpacho

·

Moroccan Carrot And
Beetroot Salad

·

Cypriot Nut Fetta Cheese

·

Maltese Caponata

Lebanese Za'atar Flat Bread

Ingredients:

4 medium zucchini (courgettes), chopped
500 g (16 oz) yellow pumpkin or butternut squash, chopped
125 g (4 oz) psyllium powder
180 g (6 oz) ground flaxmeal
1 teaspoon za'atar spice mixture (middle eastern spice available from spice merchants)
2 teaspoons sea salt
¼ teaspoon ground black pepper
water (add just enough to make the mixture moist)
sesame seeds, to serve

Method:

1. Blend the zucchini and pumpkin in a blender until smooth, and then add the balance of the ingredients.
2. Slowly add in a little of the water keeping some in reserve to adjust the consistency for spreading onto teflex sheets or baking paper. It might take you several attempts to achieve this but practice makes perfect.
3. Spread the mix into round shapes no more than 4 mm (0.15 in) thick, ensuring there are no holes. Set the dehydrator to 42.5°C (115°F) and run for 4–6 hours (or put in the oven at less than 50°C (120°F), with the fan on and door open for 2–3 hours).
4. Take care not to fully dry the flatbreads, as you need to be able to fold them. Turn at the first opportunity to keep them relatively soft and pliable.
5. Sprinkle with sesame seeds to serve.

Cauliflower Couscous

Ingredients:

½ large cauliflower

2 dessertspoons dukkah (mixed Middle Eastern dried nut and spice combination) or peanut spice (available from markets or spice shops)

1 spring onion (scallion), finely sliced

2 limes, juiced

½ preserved lemon, finely chopped (available from a delicatessen)

1 teaspoon olive oil

salt and pepper, to taste

lettuce leaf, to serve

1 dessertspoon diced red capsicum (bell pepper), for garnish

Method:

1. Chop the cauliflower into small florets and pulse in a food processor until couscous consistency is reached.
2. Turn out into a prep bowl and add the other ingredients and thoroughly mix through.
3. This can be served in your bento box on a lettuce leaf.
4. Garnish with the red capsicum.

Fattoush with Hummus

This remains one of my favorite north African recipes and as my partner Clare says; the secret to a good fattoush is in the way the garlic, oil and salt are combined in a mortar and pestle; too much of either ingredient and the true nature of the dish is lost.

Ingredients for the fattoush:

6–8 small pieces of flat bread (recipe on page 73)
6 cherry tomatoes, halved
1 red or Spanish onion, chopped roughly
1 teaspoon sumac powder (available from your spice counter)
1 Lebanese cucumber, chopped roughly
180 g (6 oz) fresh mint, chopped
125 g (4 oz) flat leaf parsley, chopped
125 g (4 oz) fresh coriander (cilantro), chopped
125 g (4 oz) olive oil
1 medium garlic clove
1 lemon, juiced
½ teaspoon salt, for use in a mortar and pestle

Ingredients for the hummus:

500 g (16 oz) sprouted chickpeas or a tin of precooked chickpeas (its OK to use the tinned version but the sprouted ones will be 100% alive)
2 dessertspoons tahini
1 zucchini (courgette), peeled
1 medium garlic clove
¼ teaspoon sweet paprika
salt and pepper, to taste

Method for the fattoush:

1. Place the cherry tomatoes, onion, sumac powder, cucumber, salt, pepper, mint, parsley and coriander in a prep bowl.
2. In a mortar and pestle, grind the garlic with a ½ teaspoon of salt to a fine paste then add the lemon juice, olive oil and pepper. You can also use the small cup on your blender and gently pulse this mixture to achieve the same outcome. Add and mix through the salad.
3. Adjust to taste with extra salt and pepper, if desired.
4. Turn onto a serving dish and add some of the fresh coriander as a garnish.

Method for the hummus:

1. Place all the ingredients in your high speed blender or food processor and blend thoroughly until thick but runny consistency.
2. Season to taste.
3. To serve you can place 3 dessertspoons of hummus onto a lettuce cup and place the fattoush on the top.

Moroccan Gazpacho

Ingredients:

4 large vine ripened tomatoes, coarsely chopped

1 extra tomato, diced for garnish

4 Lebanese cucumbers, peeled and diced

80 ml (2 ¾ fl oz) extra virgin olive oil

2 tablespoons lemon juice

2 teaspoons agave or coconut palm nectar

1 teaspoon sea salt

1 teaspoon fresh ginger, peeled and grated

¾ teaspoon cumin powder

¾ teaspoon coriander (cilantro) powder

½ teaspoon cinnamon

¼ teaspoon black pepper

⅛ teaspoon cayenne pepper

60 g (2 oz) fresh coriander (cilantro), chopped

60 g (2 oz) pine nuts

60 g (2 oz) organic raisins

Method:

1. Blend all of the ingredients, except for the diced tomato for garnish, pine nuts, raisins and fresh coriander. The mixture should be nice and creamy in texture. Add extra water if needed.
2. Stir in the diced tomato, pine nuts, raisins and shredded coriander.
3. This recipe makes about 5–6 bowls of this tasty gazpacho.
4. Serve in small bowls or glasses, as this is quite moreish.
5. Garnish with the extra-diced tomato on top and a grind of black pepper.

Moroccan Carrot and Beetroot Salad

Ingredients:

3 medium carrots, grated

1 medium beetroot, peeled and grated

125 g (4 oz) raisins

½ teaspoon paprika, sweet or smoked depending on your preference

¼ teaspoon cumin powder

¼ teaspoon cinnamon powder

¼ teaspoon of cayenne powder

2 tablespoons lemon juice

1 tablespoon agave or coconut palm syrup

2 tablespoons fresh mint leaves, chopped

salt, to taste

Method:

1. Place the grated carrots in a medium sized serving bowl. Put the grated beetroot into a sieve and briefly rinse with cold water. This will rinse away a little of the excess beetroot juice that may otherwise stain the whole salad. Dry with a paper towel. Add to the carrots in the bowl along with the raisins. Stir to gently combine.

2. In a small bowl, whisk together the paprika, cumin, cinnamon, salt and cayenne. Then add the lemon juice and agave syrup and whisk until smooth.

3. Drizzle over the carrot and beetroot and gently fold in then let sit for an hour before serving, either chilled or at room temperature. This allows the dressing to seep into the carrots and beetroot.

4. Just before serving, stir in a couple of tablespoons of sliced fresh mint leaves. Garnish with fresh mint.

5. This is nice served in an upside down empty avocado skin to ensure the red juices don't flow out everywhere.

Cypriot Nut Fetta Cheese

Ingredients:

750 g (24 oz) finely ground macadamia nuts

125 ml (4 fl oz) water

2 capsules probiotics – dairy free

3 lemons, juiced

1 teaspoon fine sea salt

Method:

1. Place the nut fines in a prep bowl and add water to just cover the top and soak for 4 hours. The nut fines will absorb the water and expand.

2. After this time has elapsed mix in the powder from the capsules of probiotics, the lemon juice and add salt to taste.

3. Stir the mixture thoroughly then spoon into a muslin cloth or a nut bag.

4. Place the bag and its contents onto a sieve and sit it over a bowl with a weight on the top.

5. Set aside on your bench top in the open air so the culture gets to work for 2–3 days. You might see some discoloration, which is quite normal and a fermentation smell will become more evident. All of this is normal and OK. After this time you can place into an airtight storage container in the fridge or make mini cheese molds using stainless steel food forms.

6. The cheese will last for 2–3 weeks if you haven't eaten it all with a few days. It is excellent on crackers.

Maltese Caponata

A very traditional Maltese dish, which can still be achieved raw as long as the eggplant (aubergine) is thoroughly soaked and marinated.

Ingredients:

1 medium eggplant (aubergine), cut into thin strips, soaked and marinated

2 lemons, juiced

2 tablespoons olive oil

2 dessertspoons apple cider vinegar

salt and pepper, to taste

4 large vine ripened tomatoes

125 g (4 oz) semi-dried tomatoes

2 medium white onions, thinly sliced

2 celery stalks, chopped

6 stuffed olives, chopped into quarters

1 tablespoon capers

Method:

1. Soak the sliced eggplant in salted water for 3–4 hours; rinse off and douse in lemon juice, 1 tablespoon olive oil, apple cider vinegar and salt and leave to sit.
2. Place fresh tomatoes and semi-dried tomatoes into your food processor along with 1 tablespoon olive oil, ½ teaspoon of sea salt and ¼ teaspoon of black ground pepper. Pulse until a coarse consistency is achieved.
3. When the eggplant is thoroughly softened through marination, place into a prep bowl along with the sliced onions, chopped celery, olives and capers. Pour the blended tomato over the top.
4. Now leave this to sit for a further 2 hours – the longer you leave this the richer it will taste as you allow for all the flavors to reveal themselves.
5. Garnish with a few of the outstanding capers.

Italian Favorites

My love affair with tomato based plant dishes continues unabated. Mixing together a beautiful sauce with freshly dehydrated tomato wedges, which add a sweetness to the sauce, is without doubt one of my more joyous food pastimes. There is nothing more attractive than having a series of small portions of beautiful Italian food together on one platter.

Menu

Pizza

•

Tomato Hemp Seed
Crackers with Low Fat
Pesto

•

Ravioli with Walnut Cheese

•

Mushroom Risotto with
Tomato Sauce

•

Easy Lasagne –
Layers of Marinated
Zucchini, Tomato Sauce
and Garlic Cashew Cream

Pizza – seed bread base with a mix of toppings

When making up your seed bread base make one or two trays into plate size circles, which can be stored and used as pizza bases. They will store in an airtight container in the fridge for up to two weeks.

Ingredients for seed bread base:

500 g (16 oz) sunflower seeds, soaked for 2 hours
125 g (4 oz) walnuts, soaked for 2 hours
2 zucchini (courgettes), peeled
125 g (4 oz) flaxmeal
½ teaspoon garlic powder, dried
1 teaspoon Italian herbs, dried
½ teaspoon salt
100 ml (3 fl oz) water

Ingredients for the tomato sauce:

2 large tomatoes
½ red capsicum (bell pepper)
125 g (4 oz) semi-dried tomatoes
1 large spring onion (scallion)
2 cloves of garlic
¼ teaspoon dried Italian herbs, or fresh basil if you have it
2 dessertspoons macadamia oil
1 dessertspoon of lime juice
salt and pepper, to taste

Ingredients for the pine nut cheese:

60–125 g (2–4 oz) pine nuts
1 lime, juiced
clove of garlic

Method for seed bread base:

1. Blend all the ingredients in an S-blade food processor gradually adding water until a stiff but damp consistency is reached. Do not make it too damp or the mixture will be difficult to roll onto your teflex paper.
2. Place approximately 2 cups of the mixture onto the teflex paper, tear off some baking paper to cover the area and using a rolling pin, roll out so it's square to the edges of the teflex.
3. Using a medium sized dinner plate, upside down, score out a circle on your mixture. You may also choose to use a smaller plate and get 2–3 bases from your mix.
4. Place in the dehydrator 43°C (115°F) and set the timer for 4 hours. After this time check for even drying and turn 'back to front' if necessary. Set timer for a further 4 hours. At this time flip the sheet over onto the mesh beneath the teflex and dry again for a further 2–3 hours.
5. Around about this time you will be able to pop the 'pizza base' out of the center of the dried sheet. The surrounding dried mix can be used for irregular sized sunflower seed crackers.
6. Pizza bases can be used straight away or stored for future use.

Method for the tomato sauce:

1. Blend all the above ingredients until course to smooth.

½ dessertspoon nutritional
   savory yeast
extra water, if needed

Ingredients for the pizza topping:

diced capsicum (bell pepper)
slithers of button mushrooms
olives, artichokes, capers
pine nut cheese (recipe
   above)
dried herbs or fresh basil
salt and pepper, as desired

Method for the pine nut cheese:

1. Blend ingredients coarsely. Add water if mixture is too thick.

Method for the pizza:

1. To assemble your pizza simply apply a layer of tomato sauce to your seed bread and top with veggies of your choice. Feel free to experiment. Top off with basil leaves filled with the pine nut cheese.

Tomato Hemp Seed Crackers with Low Fat Pesto

This makes enough for two to three trays, perhaps up to 36 snacks depending on how wide you score the crackers.

Ingredients for the tomato hemp seed crackers:

750 g (24 oz) organic sunflower seeds

250 g (8 oz) hemp seeds

250 g (8 oz) semi-dried tomato halves, diced

125 ml (4 fl oz) water

250 g (8 oz) flaxseed, soaked overnight then rinsed

salt and pepper, to season

Ingredients for the low fat pesto:

2 medium size zucchini (courgette)

500 g (16 oz) basil, fresh leaves

125 g (4 oz) parsley

125 g (4 oz) pine nuts

2 large cloves of garlic

1 dessertspoon lime juice

sprig of sage

salt and pepper, to taste

Method for the tomato hemp seed crackers:

1. Blend all ingredients apart from the flaxseeds in the order listed. Add the flaxseeds after blending then pulse a few times for a final mix. Add just enough water to create a firm – damp 'cement' like mix.
2. Take a third of the mixture and roll onto teflex sheets or baking paper getting a thickness of around 2 mm (0.1 in). Score with the back of a knife into small cracker size shapes.
3. Dehydrate for 8–12 hours turning every 3 hours and separating the snacks. You will know when they are done when they are firm and crispy.

Method for the low fat pesto:

1. Blend all the ingredients together until the mix has a smooth consistency. Taste and add extra lime juice or salt as desired. The citrus will preserve the mixture for up to 10 days. Remember this is oil free.

Ravioli with Walnut Cheese

Ingredients for the walnut cheese:

250 g (8 oz) walnuts, soaked for two hours
2 medium garlic cloves
60 ml (2 fl oz) cashew nut milk (see recipe on page 67)
2 teaspoons of nutritional savory yeast
1 dessertspoon macadamia oil
½ lime, juice
salt and pepper, to taste

Ingredients for the ravioli:

1 medium size beetroot, peeled
1 small yellow squash, peeled
120 ml (4 fl oz) macadamia oil
60 ml (2 fl oz) apple cider vinegar
60 ml (2 fl oz) agave or coconut nectar
salt and pepper, to taste

Method for the walnut cheese:

1. Combine the walnuts, garlic, cashew nut milk, savory yeast, oil, lime and seasoning. Blend thoroughly to achieve a firm to moist consistency.

Method for the ravioli:

1. Slice the beetroot and squash, thinly using a mandolin.
2. Immerse in a bowl with the liquid ingredients and add salt and pepper to taste. Allow to marinade for at least an hour
3. To make up the ravioli begin by taking a slice of beetroot and apply a teaspoon of the cheese mixture. Top with a slice of the marinaded squash. Serve each of the small raviolis on a bed of green leaves of your choice.

Mushroom Risotto with Tomato Sauce

You can vary the sauce recipe depending on what your have in your vegetable container.

Ingredients for the tomato sauce:

2 large tomatoes
½ red capsicum (bell pepper)
75 g (2.5 oz) semi-dried
   tomatoes
1 large spring onion (scallion)
2 cloves of garlic
¼ teaspoon dried Italian herbs
   (or fresh basil if you have it)
1 dessertspoon macadamia oil
1 dessertspoon lime juice
salt and pepper, to taste

Ingredients for the mushroom risotto:

4 whole large Swiss Brown or
   Portobello mushrooms
1 medium size zucchini
   (courgette)
½ Lebanese cucumber
squeeze of lime
dash of macadamia oil
salt and pepper
garlic chives, to garnish,
   chopped finely

Method for the tomato sauce:

1. Blend all the above ingredients until course to smooth.

Method for the mushroom risotto:

2. Lightly pulse the mushrooms to a rice consistency.
3. Lightly pulse the zucchini, cucumber and the rest of the ingredients.
4. On a small round sheet of greaseproof paper, use a round food form and fill with the separate vegetable mixtures to create two layers (as shown).
5. Top with the tomato sauce and garlic chives to garnish.

Easy Lasagne

Ingredients for the tomato sauce:

2 large tomatoes
½ red capsicum (bell pepper)
125 g (4 oz) semi-dried tomatoes
1 large spring onion (scallion)
2 cloves of garlic
¼ teaspoon dried Italian herbs, or fresh basil
2 dessertspoons macadamia oil
1 dessertspoon of lime juice
salt and pepper, to taste

Ingredients for the garlic cashew cream:

250 g (8 oz) of raw cashews, soaked for 2–3 hours
2 cloves of garlic
60 g (2 oz) cashew or coconut milk, or coconut cream
3–4 teaspoons of nutritional savory yeast
1 teaspoon lime juice
salt and pepper, as required

Ingredients for the lasagne:

(Modify amounts to suit)
3 large zucchini (courgettes), cut into 2cm (¾ in) strips
tomato sauce
garlic cashew cream

Method for the tomato sauce:

1. Blend all the ingredients until course to smooth.

Method for the garlic cashew cream:

1. Blend all the above ingredients until smooth.

Method for the lasagne:

1. Thinly slice the zucchini lengthwise (or across into thin circles, if your fruit is large enough) using a mandolin.

How to assemble the lasagne:

1. Place a square piece of greaseproof or baking paper on a large white plate so you can lift the lasagne into your bento box or onto your platter. Then place strips of the zucchini side by side to form a base. Add a layer of the tomato mixture. Lay down more strips of zucchini evenly across the top of the tomato. Next, spoon on a layer of the creamy cashew sauce evenly across the zucchini. Add another layer of zucchini and another layer of tomato sauce. Top off with cashew cream mix and pesto if desired (see recipe on page 90).
2. You could also sprinkle nut 'parmesan' over the top (see recipe on page 38).
3. Once your lasagne 'build' is complete, depending in the size of your zucchini strips you may like to 'square off' the sides with a sharp knife.

Asian Sensation

I am fortunate enough to have chosen to live in one of the most magnificent parts of this beautiful planet. Here all the wonderful spices used in Thai food grow in abundance – garlic, ginger, galangal, kaffir lime leaf and coriander (cilantro) – I find these spices and herbs exciting not least because of their pungency and fragrance. You will find these delightfully aromatic and tasty spices right throughout this book.

Menu

Kelp Noodles with Soused
Organic Vegetables

•

Vegetable Laksa

•

Mock 'Crab' Sweet Potato
Gnocchi

•

Thai Orange Vegetable
Salad

•

Sea Vegetable Seed
Crackers

Kelp Noodles with Soused Organic Vegetables

Ingredients for the noodles:

690 g (24 oz) cabbage, cut
  finely
345 g (12 oz) carrot, cut finely
172 g (6 oz) fresh ginger,
  peeled and sliced finely
345 g (12 oz) kelp noodles,
  soaked for 15 mins (available
  from your Asian grocer)
½ chili of choice, deseeded

Ingredients for the sauce:

¼ teaspoon fine earth salt
3 dessertspoons lime juice
2 dessertspoons Japanese rice
  wine
1-2 dessertspoons tamari,
  wheat free
1 dessertspoon sesame oil
1 dessertspoon coconut palm
  syrup

Method:

1. Place the finely sliced vegetables and chili into a plastic zip-lock bag. Cover with the salt, close the bag and begin to work the salt around the vegetables until a liquid starts to fill the bottom of the bag. At this stage, place the bag under a weight for an hour at which time you can pour off the salty liquid from the bottom. Set aside in a prep bowl.

2. In a separate bowl combine the lime juice, rice wine, tamari, sesame oil and palm syrup – add more or less tamari to achieve the balance you prefer.

3. Now add the kelp noodles to the vegetables and pour over the sauce. Stir this through the vegetables and let sit for a further 1 hour if you have the time, otherwise serve with your box immediately.

4. The longer the vegetables are left in the sauce the tastier they become. You can just add the kelp noodles at the time of preparation.

Vegetable Laksa

I have to acknowledge laksa is one of my most favorite flavor and taste combinations. It is an Asian inspired soup embodying the true essence of the orient.

Ingredients for the paste (which can be premade and stored for up to four weeks in the fridge):

4 stalks lemongrass, crushed

1 dessertspoon chopped fresh ginger

1 large clove garlic

1–3 red chili, depending on your heat preference

3 teaspoons coconut oil

1 small kaffir lime leaf, deveined

¼ teaspoon chopped galangal root

1 teaspoon coriander (cilantro), chopped

1 dessertspoon coconut nectar

60 g (2 oz) soaked cashews

⅛ teaspoon salt, to taste

several sprigs of coriander (cilantro), for garnish

extra water, if needed at time of blending

Ingredients for the soup:

prepare up to 500 g (16 oz) chopped, sliced, julienned vegetables – I enjoy the following:

broccoli

carrot

spring onion (scallion)

capsicum (bell pepper) – red and yellow

snow peas (mangetout)

350 ml (12 fl oz) organic coconut milk

2 zucchini (courgettes), peeled and spiralised into thick spaghetti creating a noodle effect

Method:

1. Place all of the paste ingredients, except water, into a high speed blender and bring down to a thick paste. Add extra water if needed.

2. Place the cut and prepared vegetables into serving bowls. Spiralise the zucchini and add to your bowls of vegetables.

3. Pour the coconut milk into the blender jug. Add 1 teaspoon of your premade laksa paste and blend thoroughly.

4. Pour this over each of your bowls of prepared noodles and vegetables. Top off with a fresh sprig of coriander.

5. This soup can also be heated in your dehydrator. It can be served in small cups or bowls which fit in your bento box presentation.

Mock 'Crab' Sweet Potato Gnocchi

Ingredients:

2 large sweet potatoes, peeled and cut into chunks

2 medium gloves of garlic

250 g (8 oz) psyllium husks

½ to 1 teaspoon salt, to taste

60 g (2 oz) dulce seaweed flakes

1 medium size pickled gherkin

1 dessertspoon finely chopped coriander (cilantro), or flat leafed parsley

250 ml (8 fl oz) water

125 g (4 oz) coconut flour (from your Asian grocer)

Method:

1. Place the chopped sweet potato into your blender along with all the ingredients except the coconut flour. Hold back on some of the water otherwise the mixture might become too wet. Add more water if needed to achieve a damp firm mix.

2. Transfer this mix to a prep bowl and slowly add in the coconut flour. Thoroughly work it into the mix.

3. Cover a small section of your bench top with a layer of the coconut flour. Take 250 g (8 oz) of the mix and roll into long 'snake-like' lengths allowing you to cut the gnocchi into about 3 cm (1.5 in) lengths.

4. Place the cut gnocchi onto a dehydrating tray and warm at 65°C (149°F) for 30 minutes.

5. Roll in olive oil or pesto (see recipe on page 90).

6. These make a great addition to any meal including the Italian Favorites simply by leaving out the seaweed and adding tomato sauce.

Thai Orange Vegetable Salad

I simply love 'throwing' vegetables together and merging them with bold flavors. I experience a sense of freedom because essentially there are no rules.

Ingredients for the salad:

1 zucchini (courgette), chopped into 2.5 cm (1 in) long matchsticks

3 medium carrots, chopped into 2.5cm (1 in) long matchsticks

½ red cabbage, sliced thinly

1 red capsicum (bell pepper), sliced thinly

2 spring onions (scallions), chopped finely

1 orange, with clean wedges removed

1 lime, juiced

2 dessertspoons coriander (cilantro), cut finely

1 sprig of coriander (cilantro), for garnish

28 g (1.3 oz) cashews, crushed for garnish

Ingredients for the dressing:

125 g (4 oz) cashews, soaked overnight

1 dessertspoon fresh ginger, peeled and chopped finely

1 garlic clove, peeled and chopped

1 dessertspoon of coconut nectar

2 limes, juiced

2 tablespoons wheat-free tamarin

¼ chili, cut finely

salt, to taste

Method:

1. Chop and combine all the vegetables and set aside in a prep bowl. Combine all the ingredients for the dressing in a small blender and blend thoroughly.

2. Pour the dressing over the vegetables and mix in the crushed cashews. Serve with a splash of coriander (cilantro) green to garnish.

Sea Vegetable Seed Crackers

Ingredients:

500 g (16 oz) hulled sunflower seeds

125 g (4 oz) buckwheat seeds, activated (soak overnight then rinse off in the morning)

125 g (4 oz) flaxmeal

125 g (4 oz) dulce seaweed, chopped finely

60 g (2 oz) sundried or semi-dried tomatoes

¼ teaspoon red chili, chopped

extra water if needed

salt and pepper, to taste

Method:

1. Blend all the ingredients together in the order listed. Pulse your blender a few times to mix the seeds together into a paste. Add just enough water to create a firm but damp paste.
2. Take a third of the mixture and roll onto teflex sheets or baking paper, getting a cracker thickness of 3 mm (1/4 in). Score with the back of a knife into small cracker size shapes.
3. Place in your dehydrator and dehydrate for 8–12 hours turning every 3 hours. At the halfway point the mix will be dry enough to begin to separate the snacks. You will know they are done when they are firm and crispy.
4. Makes enough for two to three trays, perhaps up to 36 crackers depending on how wide your score them.
5. Dulce seaweed is full of amazing nutrients. See page 15 for a breakdown.

Japanese Bento

We are staying in Asia for this menu, but
this time in Japan, the home of the bento
box. These recipes fit perfectly into a box
with some minor variations on the originals.
I know you will still enjoy them. This is the
consummate bento box.

Menu

Nigiri Sushi with Spicy
Mock Tuna Toppings

•

Cucumber Ribbons

•

Coconut Wraps with
Asian Rice

•

Raw Coconut Turmeric and
Nori Cone with Vegetables

•

Cauliflower Greens
With Ginger Sesame Sauce

Nigiri Sushi with Spicy Mock Tuna Toppings

Ingredients for the rice:

5–6 large parsnips, or firm white turnip, peeled and chopped

1 lemon, juiced

1 teaspoon apple cider vinegar

2 tablespoons cashew butter, process down using s-blades of food processor

1 tablespoon nama shoyu or wheat free tamari

salt to taste

Ingredients for the spicy mock tuna:

1 blood orange or grapefruit, remove pith and segment

¼ teaspoon cayenne pepper, to taste

1 tablespoon dulse seaweed flakes

⅛ teaspoon salt

Ingredients for toppings:

2 medium-sized tomatoes cut into quarters with center removed.

1 Lebanese cucumber, cut into fine strips 2 cm (¾ in) thick

¼ pinapple, cut into lengths

Method for the rice:

1. Pulse the chopped parsnips through a food processor until rice consistency is achieved. Blend the balance of the ingredients through the parsnip rice being careful to ensure you mixture has a firm, not wet outcome.

Method for the spicy mock tuna:

1. Marinate the grapefruit segments in the cayenne, dulse flakes and earth salt for 1–2 hours. They will be used as a topping for the sushi.

To assemble the nigiri and toppings:

1. Using a sharp knife remove the skin from the tomato revealing the flesh. Now facing down, gently 'fillet' the flesh from the tomato and shape to 'fish-like' appearance. Gently score the topside as shown in the image. This is the second topping.
2. 'Fillet' the cucumber and prepare the pineapple and broccoli.
3. Now to assemble; for nigiri rice you can use a nigiri mold available from an Asian food store or take one heaped dessertspoon of the rice mixture and using your hand fashion into bite size portions.
4. Place the spicy mock tuna grapefruit over the top of two pieces of nigiri and season with either black pepper or black sesame seeds.
5. Place the skinned tomato flesh on top of two nigiri pieces.
6. Now fix the cucumber into place by using a thin strip of nori paper to wrap around the nigiri rice.
7. Fix the pineapple in place using a thin strip of cucumber.
8. Fashion the nori paper into a container, approx. 8cm (3 in) long and 5 cm (2 in) high. Half fill with 'rice' and top off with the broccoli flowers.

2 cm (¾ in) thick

2 teaspoons finely chopped
  broccoli flowers

Ingredients to serve:

2–3 nori seaweed sheets

light greens for garnishing
  – including coriander
  (cilantro), daikon radish or
  shredded seaweed

9. Garnish with sliced Lebanese cucumber, tomato and greens. You may also like to fashion a 'fish' from finely sliced 'fillets' of daikon radish or other vegetables of choice.
10. Serve with fresh wasabi and wheat free tamari or shoyu.

Cucumber Ribbons

Here is an opportunity to use one of the blades in the very popular 3 in 1 slicer or spiraliser. It's the flat one, which creates a flat round shape as opposed to a noodle or spaghetti form.

Ingredients:

3 Lebanese cucumbers – sliced
  using the flat blade from a
  spiraliser or 3 in 1 slicer and
  set aside in the fridge with
  a squeeze of lime juice and
  a ¼ teaspoon salt

80 g (2 ¾ oz) fresh basil leaves

240 ml (8 fl oz) olive oil

¼ teaspoon salt

¼ teaspoon lime juice

Method:

1. Blend all the ingredients apart from the cucumber in a high speed blender until a thin consistency is achieved. Retrieve your cucumber from the fridge and pour off the salty water from the bottom of the bowl. Stir in half of the pesto mix and set aside the balance.

2. Add extra salt and lime juice to taste. This is an easy yet picturesque way to serve cucumber. I have found it especially nice when left in the fridge to cool down for 30 minutes or so.

Coconut Wraps with Asian Rice

There are more and more vegan coconut products emerging in the market place. Whilst I am a proponent of 'hand making' as much of my food as possible, I occasionally come across products which meet my strict criteria for freshness, chemical free and 100% vegan. Coconut wraps are now widely available in health food stores and online. and make a great easy alternative to making your own vegetable wraps. These 'pre-made' wraps are also great when you are travelling. All you need to do is to find your favorite filling and fill to your heart's content.

Here is my favorite Asian inspired filling for coconut wraps.

Ingredients:

500 g (16 oz) cauliflower florets, pulsed into rice consistency

125 g (4 oz) cashew nuts, soaked overnight

125 ml (4 fl oz) coconut milk

1 kaffir lime leaf, deveined and chopped finely

1 teaspoon fresh ginger, finely diced

2 medium cloves of garlic

¼ red capsicum (bell pepper), chopped finely

1 teaspoon coriander (cilantro), chopped

2 limes, juiced

¼ teaspoon salt

Method:

1. Blend all the ingredients except the rice until a smooth milk consistency is achieved and then hand blend in the cauliflower rice.
2. On your chopping block, lay out a wrap and evenly apply the cauli cream mixture. Now gently roll the wrap away from you.
3. Slice into three and serve. Garnish with any left over coriander. A great addition to any meal or served as a canapé to unsuspecting guests.

Raw Coconut Turmeric and Nori Cone with Vegetables

....

Raw coconut wraps can be purchased in packets of seven online for the user who becomes addicted to these morsels. They contain pure coconut meat, rolled and dried.

Ingredients:

4 coconut wraps, removed from their backing paper

4 pieces nori paper

tamari sauce

Vegetables of choice:

sliced carrot

sliced cucumber

sliced spring onion (shallot)

sliced red capsicum (bell pepper)

sliced daikon radish

sliced greens such as lettuce, kale, spinach, Asian greens

Method:

1. Place a coconut wrap onto your chopping block. Over the top place a nori paper. Cut both in half lengthwise. Now in one begin to lie vegetables down in one corner of the square. Roll to the other side forming a cone. You can fill up more of the cone if you wish and you may also choose to add some cauliflower rice. Continue until all the ingredients are used.

2. Now pour some of the tamari sauce down the center of the cone and devour. You may want to add some wasabi to your tamari to give it an added bite; either way it is a quick and simple way to get food in front of hungry friends and family.

Cauliflower Greens with Ginger Sesame Sauce

Essentially most of the cauliflower is edible especially the large firm finger-like fronds surrounding the flower. When stripping off your cauli, keep these fronds and use them.

Ingredients for the cauliflower greens:

4–6 cauliflower 'fingers', cut finely

2 medium carrots, peeled and cut finely

1 Lebanese cucumber, with center removed and cut finely

Ingredients for the ginger sesame sauce:

125 ml (4 fl oz) sesame oil, organic is preferred

½ teaspoon fresh ginger, finely diced

2 dessertspoons Japanese rice wine

1 dessertspoon coconut nectar

pinch salt, to taste

Method:

1. Bring together in your prep bowl all the prepared and cut vegetables.
2. Blend the sauce ingredients together and pour over the vegetables. Allow to sit for an hour or two so the flavors merge with the spiciness of the cauliflower fronds.
3. This can be stored in an airtight jar in the fridge for up to 10 days.

Indian Spices

Some of these recipes have featured in my previous recipe publications. The reason for including them again is because they lend themselves ideally to the Bento box culture. In traditional Indian cuisine these recipes might figure in what is called a tallee, a series of small stainless steel bowls all grouped together on a platter. When presented in a box format they take on a life of their own from an international point of view. I know you will love the combination of flavors.

Menu

White Radish Carrot Tarts
with Cardamom Puree

•

Corn and Tomato Naan
Bread

•

Cauliflower, Broccoli and
Pineapple Rice

•

Spicy Curry Waffle

•

Vegetable Bangalore Phall

•

Coconut and Coriander
Raita

•

Sweet Tomato Cumin Relish

White Radish Carrot Tarts with Cardamom Puree

Ingredients for the tart base:

250 g (8 oz) sunflower seeds

125 g (4 oz) flaxmeal

125 g (4 oz) coconut flour

125 g (4 oz) psyllium powder

1 large clove of garlic

1 teaspoon salt

250 ml (8 fl oz) water, to
moisten the mixture

Ingredients for the tart filling:

5 medium carrots, blended
with just enough water to
enable the mixture to be
strained off through a nut
bag or muslin cloth

1 blood orange, juiced

1 clove of garlic, flattened and
chopped

1 dessertspoon of macadamia
oil

salt and pepper, to taste

Ingredients for the cardamom puree:

250 g (8 oz) soaked cashews

250 ml (8 fl oz) coconut cream

½ teaspoon cardamom powder

1 clove of garlic

2 dessertspoons lime juice

¼ teaspoon ground pepper

salt to taste

Method for the tart base:

1. In your food processor blend all the dry ingredients until
   they are powder-like. Add small amounts of water to create
   a firm but moist consistency that can be moulded into a flat
   tin tart tray. Place the tray in the dehydrator at 42.5°C (115°F)
   or put in the oven at the lowest temp with the fan on and
   the door open until the tarts are firm. Push out of the tray
   and place them directly onto the mesh in your dehydrator
   or onto baking paper in the oven for another few minutes
   to firm up their bases. When you are satisfied they are
   completely dry, set them aside. This process may take
   2–4 hours.

Method for the tart filling:

1. Strain the water off the carrot mixture using a nut bag. Then
   stir the orange juice, garlic, oil and salt and pepper into the
   carrot mulch. The goal is to have a firm consistency but if
   you need to moisten the mix then add back some of the
   strained carrot juice.
2. Spoon off some of the mixture into each of your tart bases.
   Ensure the mixture is not too wet as this will make the
   bases soggy. Top off with a slice of radish and sprinkle white
   sesame seeds on the top. Serve with the cardamom puree
   (recipe below).

Method for the cardamom puree:

1. Blend all the ingredients together.
2. Serve ontop of the tarts.

Corn and Tomato Naan Bread

Ingredients for the corn bread:

250 g (8 fl oz) frozen corn – thawed

125 g (4 oz) flaxmeal

125 g (4 oz) psyllium husks

1 teaspoon heaped cumin powder

1 teaspoon salt

Ingredients for the tomato sauce:

3 large tomatoes

2 dessertspoons semi- or sun-dried tomatoes

1 clove of garlic

1 teaspoon onion powder

¼ teaspoon ground pepper

1 dessertspoon lime juice

salt to taste

Method for the corn bread:

1. Thoroughly blend all the above ingredients in a food processor ensuring the corn is completely broken down and then set aside.

Method for the tomato sauce:

1. Blend all the ingredients together and add into your already prepared dry ingredients for the corn bread. Blend until the mixture is quite firm but runny. Remember to watch for the mixture falling away from the sides of your blender. When this happens you have the right amount of psyllium, which acts as a binder and create a rubbery effect in your naan.

2. Place the equivalent of 4 dessertspoons of this damp mixture onto your teflex or baking paper and using a spatula create large, plate like circles. Place in the dehydrator for 4 hours, turning halfway. You are looking for a well bound, but bendy wrap. The outcome should be firm but spongy. In order to get the final product nicely rounded use a plate to cut around the edges.

3. These will keep in an airtight container in the fridge for up to a week. Either way they make great food packaging material.

Cauliflower, Broccoli and Pineapple Rice

Raw vegan rice can come in many forms. We know it is not a traditional 'seed based' rice grown in the paddy fields of Asia, it is simply a 'look alike', but with far more enriching health qualities. For many people traditional rice literally turns to sugar in the gut so using a vegetable alternative is a great way to still enjoy the 'rice experience' without the consequences.

Ingredients:

½ medium size cauliflower

½ teaspoon of mirin (fermented rice seasoning) or Japanese vinegar

1 spring onion (scallion) or shallot, finely chopped

125 g (4 oz) pineapple, finely chopped

125 g (4 oz) broccoli florets, finely prepared

salt, to taste

Method:

1. Pulse the cauliflower and mirin in a food processor until rice-like in consistency. Add the finely chopped shallots (spring onions). No further pulsing is required as it's important this mix doesn't become sticky and stodgy.

2. Now thoroughly blend the rice with the pineapple and broccoli. This makes either a great meal on its own or taking pride of place in your box.

Spicy Curry Waffle

We find many people love the idea of being able to pick up finger size morsels and this spicy waffle fits the bill admirably.

Ingredients:

460 g (16 oz) corn kernels, thawed frozen seems to work better than fresh

2 medium size zucchini (courgette), peeled and chopped

170 g (6 oz) flaxmeal

½ teaspoon salt

1 to 2 teaspoons mild curry powder – off the shelf versions are fine as long as they contain only fresh spices and no anticaking agents or chemicals

Method:

1. Blend the corn and zucchini first adding in the flaxmeal, salt and curry powder. Wait for the mixture to fall away from the sides of your blender before stopping. If this doesn't happen because your mixture is too wet then add slightly more flaxmeal (1 to 2 dessertspoons).

2. Then using silicon waffle molds (obtainable from a cake supplies store) fill the mold and flatten off the top using a spatula. Place in your dehydrator for 30 minutes at 65°C (149°F) and then turn out and continue to dry at 42.5°C (115°F) for 3–4 hours or until crisp and dry.

3. Serve with the other ingredients of your Indian box.

Vegetable Bangalore Phall

Traditionally one of the hottest curries, but for the purposes of this uncooked version I have toned it down somewhat. You may add or detract any of the hot ingredients to meet the capacity of your tastebuds to endure heat. Note: The use of lime juice and coconut yogurt helps to tone down the heat and add a sublime sweetness to the mix.

Ingredients:

approx. 500 g (16 oz) of mixed vegetables: cauliflower, carrot, broccoli, capsicum (bell pepper)

6 large tomatoes, chopped

3 spring onions (scallions), chopped

250 ml (8 fl oz) coconut yogurt (see page 155)

Ingredients for the sauce:

1 teaspoon ginger, pureed

1 teaspoon garlic, pureed

1 teaspoon onion powder

2 teaspoons mild curry powder

¼ teaspoon chili powder, less if you desire

1 teaspoon garam masala powder

6 medium size tomatoes, blended to a puree with: 250 g (8 oz) of sundried or semi-dried tomatoes

2 limes, juiced

red chilies, to garnish

Method:

1. Prepare the vegetables and set aside.
2. Place all the ingredients of the sauce into a blender and mix well. Add the sauce to the prepared vegetables and thoroughly mix through. Set aside for 2–4 hours to allow the flavors to merge completely with the vegetables.
3. Serve beside the rice in your box.

Coconut and Coriander Raita

Ingredients:

340 ml (12 fl oz) coconut cream
250 g (8 oz) coriander
  (cilantro), shredded
1 clove of garlic
1 fresh green chili
3 dessertspoons lime juice
salt and pepper to taste

Method:

1. Blend all the ingredients in your blender. It's as simple as that! Serve as a side to your Indian bento box and garnish with a sprig of coriander. Alternately pour over your curry.

Sweet Tomato Cumin Relish

Ingredients:

4 large heritage tomatoes,
  finely diced
½ red capsicum (bell pepper),
  finely diced
250 g (8 oz) pineapple, finely
  diced
1 red onion
1 large teaspoon cumin
  powder
¼ teaspoon turmeric, chopped
¼ teaspoon ginger, peeled and
  chopped
1 small clove of garlic,
  chopped
1 teaspoon coconut palm
  nectar
salt and pepper, to taste

Method:

1. Blend all the diced and chopped ingredients with the spices and palm nectar. Check on the taste and add a little salt and pepper if necessary. Leave to sit in the fridge for a few hours to enable all the flavors to merge with each other. Serve with your curry.

Vegan Cheese Board

Vegan nut cheeses are truly to live for.
Nut cheese methods and ingredients
have improved over the years with some
outcomes so resembling 'dairy cheeses', the
difference is barely discernible. I love the
smooth consistency of nut cream cheeses
especially when blended with fresh herbs
like dill or the smoky fragrance of a smoked
sweet pepper spice. A good nut cheese will
fool even the most seasoned cheese snob.

Menu

Spicy Seed Crackers

•

Cashew and Walnut Cheese
With Olives and Semi-dried
Tomatoes

•

Macadamia Cheese with
Cracked Pepper or Pesto

•

Fat Free Pesto

•

Raw Philli
Cream of Cashew and
Coconut Cheese

•

Raw Garlic Bread

Spicy Seed Crackers

Ingredients:

500 g (16 oz) soaked flax
seeds (soak the flax seeds
overnight, then rinse off
the next morning. The
residue will have become
quite gelatinous but this
is nothing to worry about.
Rinse under fresh cold
water.)

500 g (16 oz) activated
buckwheat (soak the
buckwheat overnight and
rinse off next morning)

80 g (2.8 oz) sunflower seeds,
hulled

½ dessertspoon of organic
shoyu

extra cold water, if required to
form a paste

cracked pepper, to taste

Method:

1. Blend the ingredients in the order listed pulsing the blender
   several times to mix the seeds together into a paste. Add
   more sunflower seeds if mix is too moist.

2. Take a third of the mixture at a time and roll onto teflex
   sheets to obtain a cracker thickness of around 3 mm (1/4 in).
   Score with the back of a knife into small cracker size shapes.

3. Dehydrate for 8–12 hours turning every 3 hours and
   separating the snacks. You will know they are done when
   they are firm and crispy.

4. Makes enough for two to three trays perhaps up to 36
   crackers depending on how wide you score them.

5. These are a prerequisite for your cheese set.

Cashew and Walnut Cheese with Olives and Semi-Dried Tomatoes

Ingredients:

500 g (16 oz) soaked cashews

1 dessertspoon lime juice

2 dessertspoon water

2 capsules dairy free probiotic powder (lactobacillus, acidophilus, bifobacterium lactis)

60 g (2 oz) green or black olives, pitted

60 g (2 oz) semi-dried tomatoes

60 g (2 oz) walnuts, chopped

salt to taste

Method:

1. Blend the cashews, lime juice and probiotic powder. Add salt to taste and more water if the mix appears dry. Once the mixture is pulpy, remove from the blender and spoon into a nut bag or muslin cloth. Tie the bag off and place into a sieve over a bowl with a weight on the top (I use a glass jar with water) and let sit at room temperature for a full day to allow the probiotic to work. I also put the mix into the sun or warm place to accelerate the process. Normally 24 hours in the warmth is sufficient to activate the culture.

2. Remove the mix, place in a bowl and stir through then put the mix in a food form and place in the dehydrator for 4–6 hours until you see a firm outer skin. Chop the walnuts, olives and semi-dried tomatoes and place on top of the cheese. Store in an airtight container and serve to unexpected guests or use yourself as a lovely addition to a salad or with some crackers.

Macadamia Cheese with Cracked Pepper or Pesto

Ingredients:

500 g (16 oz) soaked
  macadamia fines (finely
  chopped nuts soaked for a
  few hours in 60 ml (2 fl oz)
  water – not too soggy)
1 dessertspoon lime juice
2 cloves of garlic
2 dessertspoons water
2 capsules of dairy
  free probiotic powder
  (lactobacillus, acidophilus,
  bifobacterium lactis) or
  similar culture
salt, to taste

Method:

1. Blend the macadamia fines, garlic, lime juice and probiotic powder. Add salt to taste and a little more water if the mix appears dry. Once the mixture is pulpy, remove from the blender and spoon into a nut bag or muslin cloth. Tie the bag off and place into a sieve over a bowl with a weight on the top, I use a glass jar with water. Let sit at room temperature for a full day to allow the probiotic to work. I also put the mix into the sun or warm place to accelerate the process.

2. After 24 hours, remove the mix from the bag and 'form' the cheese using a stainless steel food form. Spoon into the form a layer of nut mixture, then add a layer of pesto (see recipe below) and add another layer of cheese mixture. Place in the dehydrator for 4–6 hours until a firm outer skin forms. Store in an airtight container until ready to use. You can also top off with more pesto or serve it separately with crackers.

3. You may also choose to layer the cheese with cracked pepper. Either way, this a great addition to your cheese board.

Fat Free Pesto

Ingredients:

2 medium size zucchini (courgettes)

500 g (16 oz) basil, chopped

125 g (4 oz) parsley

125 g (4 oz) pine nuts

2 large cloves of garlic

1 dessertspoon of lime juice

3 leaves of sage

salt, for seasoning

Method:

1. Blend all the ingredients together until the mix is a smooth consistency. This can be stored in the refrigerator for up to a week.

'Raw-Philli' – Cream of Cashew and Coconut Cheese

This is one of my favorite raw nut cheeses and I just love it's creaminess and versatility either on a seed cracker, in a wrap or just on its own.

Ingredients:

500 g (16 oz) soaked cashews

340 ml (12 fl oz) organic coconut cream

1 dessertspoon coconut oil, melted

¼ teaspoon salt

1 teaspoon lime juice

2 capsules of dairy free probiotic powder (lactobacillus, acidophilus, bifobacterium lactis)

Method:

1. Combine all the ingredients in your blender until pulpy in consistency. Set mixture in a bowl for 6–12 hours at room temperature. Remove after this time and drop into a food form and place in the fridge for a further 24 hours to firm up. Once it has become firm you can remove from the form to serve or to store in an airtight container in the fridge.

Raw Garlic Bread

A unique way to create an entirely 'wheat free bread'. This is a nutritionally dense bread and for that reason I always make my rolls quite small – about the size of half the width of the palm of my hand, flattened out.

Ingredients:

250 g (8 oz) almond flour (you may choose to grind your own)

250 g (8 oz) buckwheat flour (you may choose to grind your own)

250 g (8 oz) psyllium husks

125 g (4 oz) flaxmeal (ground linseed)

250 g (8 oz) zucchini (courgette), chopped

3 tablespoons water

3 tablespoons lemon juice

4 large garlic cloves

3 dates, pitted and soaked

1 teaspoon salt

Method:

1. Combine the zucchini, water, lemon juice, garlic cloves and dates in a high-speed blender and blend until smooth.
2. Combine almond flour, buckwheat flour, Psyllium husks, flaxmeal, onion powder, oregano and salt in a large bowl. Add the wet blended zucchini and mix through well. The mixture should be firm but pliable.
3. Form into small loaves or flat breads. Dehydrate at 42.5°C (115°F) for 14 hours.
4. It will keep for seven days in the refrigerator. Ideal when simply broken in half and cheese spread over it.

Guilt-free Desserts

Often the traditional Japanese bento box will contain an article of sweetness from a piece of fruit to a pudding or sweet bun. I have put together a small menu of sweets, which I find not only serve to cleanse the pallet but also become a small treat for the day. Obviously because they are mainly frozen they are better made and eaten at home but if you are out and about then a small chilled box is a great transport method.

Menu

Banana Ice-Cream Sandwich

•

Chocolate Cardamom Grenache cake
with Fresh Raspberries

•

Sesame – Macadamia Halva

•

Cacao and Almond Truffles
with Coconut Yogurt and Strawberry Coulis

•

Go Nuts Raw Doughnut

•

Yummy Carrot Slice

•

Orange Blossom Coconut Ice

•

Mango Cream Torrone with Fresh Coconut

•

Coconut Cashew Zabaglione
with Seasonal Fruit

•

Lime and Strawberry Granitas

•

Pumpkin Custard with Strawberry Coulis

Banana Ice-Cream Sandwich

This requires approx. 6x6 cm (2.3x2.3 in) square sectioned silicone mold or metal cake tin, or you can use a loaf style tin which will require cutting the sandwiches by hand once frozen.

Ingredients for the base:
500 g (16 oz) coconut flakes
16 medjool dates, pitted
4 tablespoons coconut oil, melted
125 g (4 oz) flaxmeal (ground linseeds)
1 teaspoon cinnamon
¼ teaspoon salt
1 teaspoon vanilla essence
1 teaspoon coconut syrup

Ingredients for the ice-cream:
4 frozen bananas
3 tablespoons almond butter
2 tablespoons dried banana, finely chopped
1 teaspoon vanilla essence
1 teaspoon coconut syrup

Method for the base:
1. Combine the ingredients in your processor. Place 1 tablespoon of the mix into the mold or tin and press firmly into the base, it should be about 5 mm (0.2 in) thick, repeat till all bases are covered or alternatively if using a loaf tin press ½ the mixture firmly over the base. Place in freezer until frozen.

Method for the ice-cream sandwich:
2. Blend bananas and almond butter together then hand mix in the finely chopped dried banana pieces.
3. Remove bases from freezer and gently remove ½ from the molds, these will become the tops of the sandwiches. If using a loaf tin roll out remaining base mixture to fit into top of tin and place in freezer to firm.
4. When you are ready to bring together, pour 60 g (2 oz) of the ice-cream mix onto the bases in the mold then place back into the freezer. Conversely pour all the ice-cream mix over the chilled base in the loaf tin.
5. Wait till the ice-cream is touch set then place the tops onto the ice-cream and gently press down. Return to freezer until frozen solid.
6. Remove from molds or if using loaf tin cut with hot knife into preferred sizes and wrap individually in baking paper to store.

Chocolate Cardamom Ganache Cake with Fresh Strawberries

··

Ingredients for the base:

250 g (8 oz) macadamia flour (macadamia pieces ground down)

250 g (8 oz) medjool dates, pitted and chopped

¼ teaspoon desert salt

Ingredients for the cake:

1-2 soft avocados

125 g (4 oz) cacao powder

60 g (2 oz) coconut oil, melted

125 g (4 oz) coconut palm crystals or coconut palm syrup

1 ½ teaspoons vanilla essence

⅛ teaspoon ground cardamom spice

½ teaspoon tamari

⅛ teaspoon salt

Method for the base:

1. In a food processor blend the macadamia nuts into flour. Add the dates, salt and blend until a dough like consistency is achieved.
2. Line a spring form pan with cling film and press the dough into the bottom. Place it in the freezer to harden until the ganache is prepared.

Method for the cake:

1. Place all the filling ingredients in a food processor and blend everything until smooth. Pour the ganache over the macadamia base and smooth off the top. Set in the freezer for 1–1.5hrs when it will be ready for removing from the spring form and slicing.
2. Serve topped with fresh strawberries.

Sesame – Macadamia Halva

Ingredients:

750 g (24 oz) sesame seeds, raw

125 g (4 oz) macadamia fines

60 g (2 oz) coconut nectar

½ teaspoon vanilla extract

¼ teaspoon desert salt

1 teaspoon currents

Method:

1. Using the dry blades of your blender or coffee grinder render the sesame seeds down to a near paste.
2. Place in a prep bowl and add the macadamia fines and other ingredients. Thoroughly blend together and taste for desired sweetness.
3. Turn out in a greaseproof lined tray and flatten off to the sides.
4. Place into the fridge overnight to allow the mix to firm.
5. Turn out the next day onto a serving dish, garnish with loose sesame seeds and cut into bite size squares.
6. You may also make bite size balls from the mix too and roll in the sesame seeds.
7. This is very filling small dessert so make sure the pieces aren't too large.
8. Serve with slices of fresh orange.

Cacao and Almond Truffles with Coconut Yogurt and Strawberry Coulis

Ingredients:
250 g (8 oz) skin-on almonds

250 g (8 oz) medjool dates, pitted

1 dessertspoon raw cacao powder

2 dessertspoons coconut palm syrup

Ingredients for the coconut yogurt and strawberry coulis:
700 ml (24 fl oz) coconut cream

6 capsules of dairy free probiotic

500 g (16 oz) hulled strawberries

This recipe can be made either with fresh coconut flesh and water, or a good quality organic coconut cream. Prepare the equivalent of 700 ml (24 fl oz) of coconut cream.

Method:
1. Using a food processor, thoroughly blend all the ingredients to a sticky but course texture. If the mixture is too dry you can either add a couple more dates or another dessertspoon of coconut syrup. Once the desired consistency has been obtained, stop the processor making sure to clear the sides.
2. To roll into truffles, simply take a teaspoon of the mixture and, using your clean hand, roll into a ball. Place in a mini paper pastry cases ready for the strawberry coulis.

Method for the coconut yogurt and strawberry coulis:
1. Empty the coconut cream into one large clean glass jar.
2. Stir in the powder from probiotic capsules (twist the ends of the capsules to open) thoroughly whisking the powder through the coconut cream.
3. Set aside in a warm space with the top covered with muslin cloth for 3-4 days until the mixture takes on a yogurt consistency and taste.
4. Once you see the cream start to thicken, pop the jar into the fridge for a few hours and it will firm up even more, taking on a yogurt like consistency. This will keep in the fridge for up to a week.
5. Pulse the strawberries in a small blender to create your coulis. Serve individual portions of yogurt and a teaspoon or two of strawberry coulis over the top of the cacao and almond balls.
6. Add to a morning fruit salad, smoothies or mixed with your favorite fruit coulis. The yogurt will firm even more when it is stored in the fridge.

Go Nuts Raw Doughnut

Makes 20 doughnuts

Ingredients:
370 g (12 oz) cashews
150 g (4 oz) desiccated
coconut
370 g (12 oz) almond pulp –
damp but not wet
2 tablespoons psyllium husks
2 teaspoons cinnamon
125 g (4 oz) coconut sugar
6 medjool dates – pitted
½ teaspoon salt
rind of 1 lemon
1 teaspoon vanilla bean
powder

Ingredients for the icing:
2 tablespoons cashews –
soaked overnight
4 tablespoons coconut nectar
2 ½ tablespoons lemon juice
¼ teaspoon sea salt
1 teaspoon vanilla essence
2 tablespoons coconut oil
2 tablespoons coconut butter
2 teaspoon lecithin

Method:
1. Blend the cashews and coconut in a processor until fine. Add the rest of the ingredients and process into a smooth dough.
2. Press into silicon doughnut mold to shape at the same time shaping the hole in the center.
3. Place in freezer for 15 minutes before removing from mold. You can alternately fashion into a doughnut shape using your hands.

Method for the icing:
1. Blend the cashews, syrup, lemon, salt and vanilla until completely smooth.
2. Add the coconut oil and coconut butter and re-blend.
3. Remove doughnut from the freezer and flip out of the mold. Then one by one dip the tops of the doughnut into the icing or alternately drizzle icing over the top with a spoon.
4. Add your favorite topping and place into the fridge to firm up before serving.

Suggested toppings:
- Desiccated coconut
- Chopped nuts
- Hemp seed
- Coconut sugar
- Cinnamon
- Fruit

Yummy Carrot Slice

Ingredients:

500 g (16 oz) walnuts

15 medjool dates, pitted

1 ¼ kg (40 oz) carrots, grated medium to fine and patted dry

250 g (8 oz) almond flour

250 g (8 oz) desiccated coconut

1 ½ teaspoons cinnamon

1 teaspoons nutmeg

1 teaspoon fresh ginger, grated

zest from 1 lemon

60 g (2 oz) sultanas

50 g (1 ¾ oz) walnut pieces

½ teaspoon salt

Ingredients for the cashew cream icing:

500 g (16 oz) cashews, soaked for 3–4 hours

2 tablespoons coconut milk

80 ml (2 ¾ fl oz) coconut palm syrup

2 teaspoons vanilla essence

juice of 1 lemon

2 teaspoons grated ginger

¼ teaspoon salt

125 ml (4 fl oz) coconut oil, melted to a liquid

Ingredients for nut topping:

12 whole walnuts

80 ml (2 ¾ fl oz) coconut palm syrup

½ teaspoon cinnamon

2 dessertspoons coconut palm sugar (crystals)

Method:

1. Blend the walnuts and dates until a just chunky consistency is achieved.

2. Place these in a large prep bowl and hand mix in the carrots, almond flour, coconut, spices, zest, sultanas, walnut pieces and salt – work thoroughly together.

3. Place firmly into a flat-sided baking tin and place in the freezer until set.

Method for the cashew cream icing:

1. Blend the cashews, coconut milk, coconut syrup, vanilla, lemon juice, ginger and salt until very smooth. Add coconut oil and blend. Pour over the frozen carrot base and re-freeze.

For the nut topping:

1. Wet whole walnut pieces in watery coconut syrup (add 2 tablespoons of warm water to the syrup to thin it down) and coat in a mix of cinnamon and coconut palm sugar, place in dehydrator until caramelized.

2. For the finish – remove the entire frozen ingredients from the backing dish by turning the dish upside down and popping it out. Better still if you have a spring form container where you can pop the frozen cake up and out of the container. Cut to individual slices and add the nut topping.

Orange Blossom Coconut Ice

Ingredients:
250 g (8 oz) raw cashews, soaked overnight
250 g (8 oz) fresh or soaked desiccated coconut
250 g (8 oz) coconut cream
62 ml (2 fl oz) coconut oil
½ teaspoon orange blossom water
2 dessertspoons coconut palm nectar sugar, or to taste
1 dessertspoon juice from mulched beetroot

Method:
1. Blend all the ingredients except the beetroot juice at high speed in your blender. Into a flat bottom, lined slice tray, pour off half of the mix. Make sure it's nice and level and place in the freezer for 20-30 minutes. To the balance of the mix add some of the beetroot color to create a lovely pink hue. Blend this thoroughly.
2. Take the now firm cream color mix from the freezer and pour in the remainder of the now pink mix. Level off to the edges. Replace the tray in the freezer for a further 20 minutes or until firm, but not frozen. Remove the firm mix from the tray and cut into squares. Place in an airtight container and store in the fridge ready for pride of place in your plate.

Mango Cream Torrone with Fresh Coconut

Ingredients:
4 mango cheeks – fresh or frozen
2 bananas – frozen
½ teaspoon lime zest, to taste
cacao nibs for garnish
grated fresh coconut or sprinkle dried coconut to taste
125 ml (4 fl oz) cashew milk, soak nuts overnight and blend next morning adding clean fresh water to achieve a milk consistency

Method:
1. Blend the mango and banana and add the lime zest until the mix is of a thick yogurt texture. Place in the freezer for 15 minutes to get the mixture to firm up.
2. In a dessert bowl or flat plate, use a food form to fill to the desired height.
3. Shake the fresh coconut over the top and pour cashew milk around the bowl and serve. This is great for an in-home box offering to family and friends.

Coconut Cashew Zabaglione with Seasonal Fruit

....

The first three ingredients also form the basis for your raw philli cream coconut cheese or alternately reduce the following ingredient list by 50% for smaller portions.

Ingredients:

500 g (16 oz) cashews, soaked overnight

340 ml (12 fl oz) organic coconut cream

(Alternately you can create your own coconut cream by using the flesh of a fresh coconut blended with the water to create a cream)

1 dessertspoon coconut oil-melted

½ teaspoon of vanilla essence

¼ teaspoon salt

125 ml (4 fl oz) coconut syrup

Seasonal fruit of your choice

Method:

1. Blend the soaked cashews, coconut cream, oil and sea salt. (If you are doing raw philli cheese then retain enough of this mixture and set aside). Combine the balance of the ingredients except the fruit until the mix is free flowing in your blender. Taste to ensure you have a level of sweetness you desire. Pour into individual serving glasses and top off with the fruit coulis that you have created in your personal 2-cup blender by adding fruit and zapping until liquefied.

Lime and Strawberry Granitas

Ingredients:

500 g (16 oz) frozen lime juice cubes

500 g (16 oz) frozen strawberries

3 dessertspoons coconut palm nectar crystals

½ teaspoon of lime zest (grated lime skin)

Method:

1. Place all the ingredients in your blender and let it rip until the cubes break down to a smooth edible form. Serve in small glasses and garnish with the lime zest. Serve with a dash of tequila if you wish!

Pumpkin Custard with Strawberry Coulis

Ingredients:

250 g (8 oz) pumpkin, peeled and chopped

250 g (8 oz) raw cashews, soaked overnight

250 ml (8 fl oz) coconut cream

¼ teaspoon cinnamon

⅛ teaspoon nutmeg shavings

⅛ teaspoon vanilla

3-4 desertspoons coconut palm nectar, to taste

2 dates, pips removed

pinch salt

water as required

500 g (16 oz) fresh or frozen strawberries, for the coulis

2 teaspoons sesame seeds, for garnish

Method:

1. Blend together the ingredients except the strawberries. Start by adding small amount of water until custard consistency is reached. Test for taste and sweetness. You are looking for a custard appeal with a slight tinge of cinnamon.

2. In your blender add the strawberries and blend until liquid. Serve the custard in small classes with the coulis on top. Top off with a sprinkle of sesame seeds.

3. Great served in your box with sweets in a small cup or shot glass.

Sauces

Raw plant based sauces are easily made and can keep up to 10 days when refrigerated. I enjoy a number of basic sauce options from white through to red and some shades in between – red capsicum (bell pepper) adds a lovely sweet pink tinge to white sauces. They can be mixed through vegetables or placed into a small container beside the vegetables in your box.

Garlic Aioli

This is an old standby for our household. Clare is a dab hand at whipping up an aioli so I will use a little chef's license and pinch her approach.

Ingredients:
225 g (8 oz) cashews – soaked overnight (so they become really creamy when blended)
juice of 4 lemons
4 large cloves garlic
125 ml (4 fl oz) coconut cream
extra water if required
salt to taste

Method:
1. Blend all the ingredients and add extra lemon juice if you want your cream to have a slight sourness to it.

The No-Fish Sauce

This rather tidy wee alternative to actual fish sauce works a treat but here is a tip: this sauce is all about your taste and flavor preferences so experiment the first few times you make it.

Ingredients:
60 g (2 oz) Dulse seaweed flakes
1 ½ limes, juiced
1-2 dessertspoons agave OR 1 to 2 dessertspoons of coconut palm syrup
½ medium red chili
1 teaspoon of sea salt, to taste

Method:
1. Blend all the ingredients and set aside ready to use. The seaweed will impart its flavor to the sauce and you can experiment with the sweetness. This will store well for up to a week in the fridge and is great for all occasions.

Creamy Coconut with Kaffir Lime

A touch of Asia is so easy to achieve with this delightful combination of spices and flavors. I use this simple sauce a lot in my GoVegan Deli. It works well with virtually any vegetable

Ingredients:

flesh from one ripe avocado

125 ml (4 fl oz) coconut cream (the canned variety is ok as long as it is free of preservatives)

1 teaspoon apple cider vinegar

1 dessertspoon olive oil

1 dessertspoon lemon juice

1 small garlic clove

1 teaspoon fresh ginger, chopped

1 kaffir lime leaf, stem removed

¼ teaspoon galangal, chopped

60 g (2 oz) coriander (cilantro), chopped finely

salt and pepper, to taste

Method:

1. Blend the ingredients until a creamy consistency is achieved. By adding slightly more lemon or lime the cream will last up to 10 days if refrigerated.

Pineapple Chili Dressing

Bringing 'warm-hot' flavors into a salad dressing is a delightful way for you and your guests to experience a little of the tropics in your salad box.

Ingredients:
2 birdseye or Jamaican chilies (or chili of choice), coarsely chopped OR
2 teaspoons of dried chili flakes
2 medium garlic cloves, coarsely chopped
250 g (8 oz) fresh sweet pineapple, diced into small pieces
juice of 3 limes
salt and pepper, to taste

Method:
1. Combine all ingredients in small 2-cup blender and blend for 15-20 seconds.

Avocado Cream

This is a nut-free sauce so is ideal for use in a school lunch where there is a anti-nut school policy. Avocado adds a wonderful creamy outcome to sauces.

Ingredients:
flesh from two ripe avocados
125 g (4 oz) zucchini, peeled
1 teaspoon apple cider vinegar
1 dessertspoon olive oil
1 dessertspoon lemon juice
1 small garlic clove (optional)
salt and pepper, to taste

Method:
1. Blend the ingredients until a creamy consistency is achieved. You may choose to add a ¼ teaspoon of your favorite curry powder to the mixture to add a different taste dimension.
2. By adding slightly more lemon or lime the cream will last up to 10 days in the fridge.

Sweet and Sour Sauce

I just love that hint of Asia in my food. Most of the ingredients used are rich in nutritional goodness.

Ingredients:

2 cloves of garlic

½ teaspoon fresh ginger

¼ teaspoon fresh galangal

60 g (2 oz) finely chopped pineapple

60 g (2 oz) macadamia oil

30 g (1 oz) nama shoyu (wheat free tamari will suffice too)

1 whole medium red chili

1 dessertspoon coconut palm syrup

1-2 limes, juiced (to taste)

¼ teaspoon desert salt

¼ teaspoon ground black pepper

Method:

1. Blend all the ingredients until thoroughly broken down. Do a final taste test and serve either in a side dish inside your box or pour over a wrap, salad or noodles.

Spicy Tomato Sauce

I almost daily have something with tomato. This sauce is so easy and with a good squeeze of lime or lemon to act as a natural preservative.

Ingredients:
3 large tomatoes

125 g (4 oz) semi- or sun-dried tomatoes

2 teaspoon mixed Italian herbs

2 cloves of garlic, crushed

1 teaspoon cayenne pepper

1 teaspoon cumin powder

1 teaspoon dried coriander OR 125 g (4 oz) fresh coriander

1 teaspoon smoked paprika

½ teaspoon salt

¼ teaspoon ground pepper

1 dessertspoon lime juice

Method:
1. Blend all the ingredients until smooth. If you want a specially thick and rich sauce then feel free to add more semi-dried tomatoes. Note also that the addition of the lime juice will further help to prolong the life of the sauce. Can be kept refrigerated for up to seven days.

Mushroom Sauce

When I am called upon to do a raw food talk and demonstration I will often do my famous Mushroom Stroganoff. This I do by simply making this sauce and adding either whole marinated button mushrooms or sliced field mushrooms. Throw in half a handful – 125 g (4 oz) of chopped flat leaf parsley and you have a simple and very tasty meal.

Ingredients:

125 g (4 oz) cashews, soaked for 3-4 hours

125 ml (4 fl oz) coconut cream

1 dessertspoon apple cider vinegar

1 small clove of garlic

1 dessertspoon mushroom powder OR two whole medium-sized dried mushrooms

1 dessertspoon olive oil

juice of 1 lime

¼ teaspoon salt and pepper, to taste

Method:

1. Blend the ingredients until thick and creamy. Taste test and add any extra if desired. In a separate bowl now, simply add some marinated mushrooms, stir in and serve over cauliflower rice.

About the author

Scott Mathias is a raw food chef, author and proprietor of the GoVegan Deli, an all vegan and plant based food store in his home town.

He maintains good health by living a plant based lifestyle which he adopted after a major digestive crisis. For many years he suffered from chronic digestive issues but with the use of natural healing aids and his raw vegan lifestyle, he completely healed.

He enjoys talking with people about healthy food options available and is often called on for talks and raw vegan demonstrations.

"The way to good health free of pain is via the gut – not just efficient function but also having an awareness of the food we eat – live food for a living body."

When not attending to his interests he enjoys nature and water. He shares his world with partner in life, Clare Darwish.

For more information on Scott's work go to:
www.scottmathiasraw.com
Facebook: scottmathiasraw
Instagram: scottmathiasraw

Bibliography for links and more information

Mushrooms: http://articles.mercola.com/sites/articles/archive/2013/05/13/mushroom-benefits.aspx

Spinach: http://www.whfoods.com/genpage.php?tname=foodspice&dbid=43

Cauliflower: http://articles.mercola.com/sites/articles/archive/2014/02/22/cauliflower-health-benefits.aspx

Carrots: http://www.care2.com/greenliving/10-benefits-of-carrots.html

Cabbage: http://www.medicalnewstoday.com/articles/284823.php

Red Cabbage: http://healthyeating.sfgate.com/health-benefits-red-cabbage-vs-green-cabbage-5647.html

Tomatoes: http://www.nutrition-and-you.com/tomato.html

Cacao: http://www.movenourishbelieve.com/nourish/pick-of-the-week-benefits-of-cacao/

Almonds: http://www.nutrition-and-you.com/almonds.html

Coconut: http://authoritynutrition.com/top-10-evidence-based-health-benefits-of-coconut-oil/

Strawberries: http://www.webmd.com/diet/nutritional-benefits-of-the-strawberry

Nutritional Yeast: http://www.livestrong.com/article/263528-what-are-the-benefits-of-nutritional-yeast-flakes/

Endnotes

[1] http://www.theguardian.com/lifeandstyle/wordofmouth/2015/jul/21/food-presentation-dinner-food-enjoyable

Index

Nueces Molidas (Walnuts in Tomato Sauce) 51

Orange Blossom Coconut Ice 159

Pineapple Chili Dressing 168
Pizza 86
Pumpkin Custard with Strawberry Coulis 162

Quick Carrot Kimchi 26

Ravioli with Walnut Cheese 91
Raw Coconut Turmeric and Nori Cone
  with Vegetables 117
Raw Garlic Bread 145
'Raw-Philli' – Cream of Cashew and Coconut
  Cheese 144
Red and White Cabbage Noodles in Asian
  Kaffir Lime Sauce 29

Sauces
  Avocado Cream 168
  Creamy Coconut with Kaffir Lime 167
  Garlic Aioli 166
  Mushroom 171
  No-Fish Sauce, The 166
  Pineapple Chili Dressing 168
  Spicy Tomato 170
  Sweet and Sour Sauce 169
Sea Vegetable Seed Crackers 106
Sesame – Macadamia Halva 153
Sour Nut Cream 52
Spicy Corn Salsa 46
Spicy Curry Waffle 129
Spicy Pickled Vegetables 61

Spicy Seed Crackers 138
Spicy Tomato Sauce 170
Spicy Vegetable Wraps with Peanut
  Dipping Sauce 62
Sweet and Sour Sauce 169
Sweet Tomato Cumin Relish 132

Thai Orange Vegetable Salad 105
Tomato and Carrot Sushi Wrap 63
Tomato Hemp Seed Crackers with Low Fat
  Pesto 90
Vegetable Bangalore Phall 130
Vegetable Laksa 102
Vine Ripened Tomatoes with Kaffir Lime
  Cream Cheese 34

White Radish Carrot Tarts with
  Cardamom Puree 124
Yummy Carrot Slice 158
Zarangollo – 'No Roast' Capsicum
  with Pimento 49
Zucchini and Corn Tortillas 52
Zucchini Noodle and Coriander Salad with
  Pineapple Chili Dressing 37

First published in 2016 by New Holland Publishers Pty Ltd
London • Sydney • Auckland

The Chandlery Unit 704, 50 Westminster Bridge Road, London SE1 7QY, United Kingdom
1/66 Gibbes Street, Chatswood, NSW 2067, Australia
5/39 Woodside Ave, Northcote, Auckland 0627, New Zealand

www.newhollandpublishers.com

A record of this book is held at the British Library and the National Library of Australia.

ISBN: 9781742578545

Managing Director: Fiona Schultz
Publisher: Linda Williams
Project Editor: Anna Brett
Designer: Lorena Susak
Photographer: Phill Jackson
Food Stylist: Jaime Reyes
Production Director: Olga Dementiev
Printer: Toppan Lefung Printing

10 9 8 7 6 5 4 3 2 1

Keep up with New Holland Publishers on Facebook
www.facebook.com/NewHollandPublishers